Astrology for Beginners

Planets, Aspects, Interpretations and Backgrounds

Contact: www.HarryEilenstein.de
Harry.Eilenstein@web.de
Harry Eilenstein at youtube

Production and publishing house: BoD – Books on Demand, Norderstedt

ISBN: 9783754305980

Table of Contents

I Foundation

Astrology is probably the best known oracle and also one of the best known parts of magic. It is connected with most mythological, magical and spiritual world views. It also has some connections to the modern physical worldview.

So it is worth to have a closer look at astrology if you are interested in magic, esotericism, occultism or more generally in worldviews that go beyond physics.

I 1. Basis: Analogy

Astrology is a system of analogies – physics is a system of causalities. So both are fundamentally different, but not contradictory – both worldviews can be combined.

Astrology considers the common quality of things that happen simultaneously – physics considers the quantitative relations of things that happen one after the other.

Astrology describes the quality of the moment – physics describes the quantitative transformation in the course of time.

So you cannot explain astrology in terms of physics and you cannot explain physics in terms of astrology. However, one can combine both worldviews to arrive at a more complete description of the world.

In astrology it is important to clearly distinguish the zodiac and the planets: The zodiac is a universal structure – the planets are an individual sequence of qualities in our solar system.

The zodiac is the division of space into 12 equal areas with a precise inner structure: 4 elements in 3 dynamics each result in 12 qualities.

This 12-structure is found in physics in two places: on the one hand in the 4 basic elementary particles (up-quark, down-quark, electron, neutrino), which appear in 3 sizes and thus have 12 forms, and on the other hand in the form of the superstring, which is divided into 12 equal areas in the same way as the zodiac and which is the basic building block of today's physics.

Moreover, the astrological aspects are also derived from the zodiac, that is, the angles and their meaning. The astrological quality of these angles is also found in physics: the 180° angle is an opposition, the 120° angle a connection, the 60° angle a grouping, the 90° angle a separation and so on.

In contrast, the meaning of the planets is relative in relation to the observer. This can be easily seen if you imagine that someone is born on Mars – then Mars drops out of the horoscope. Possibly the earth could take over the role of Mars … But then there would be the problem that also the Earth-Moon falls away, but the two Mars-Moons are added. But what if someone is born on Venus now? Should the Earth then take over the role of Venus in the horoscope – although it would have to take over the role of Mars in the case of someone born on Mars? And Venus has also no moons which could take the place of the earth moon. Finally it becomes a bit difficult, if e.g. someone is born on the Saturn moon Titan – then suddenly the 82 Saturn moons appear in the horoscope …

So there are at least three levels in astrology, which one should distinguish meaningfully:

1. the universal principle of **analogy**, which astrology shares with magic, Kabbalah, Tarot, I Ging, mythology etc.s;

2. the universal principle of the **zodiac** and the quality of some angles that can be derived from it, which can also be found in physics, Feng Shui, Kabbalah, crop circles, etc.; and

3. the **planets**, which are a relative system and refer to the Earth – for every other planet and also for every other solar system this astrological system has to be researched anew.

I 2. Types of Astrology

The most popular form of astrology today originates from Europe and is widely used, especially in Western civilization. It describes qualities: With Mars on the ascendant, one tends to be choleric.

In India there is a similar form of astrology, but it makes different statements than European astrology. It is more like medieval astrology and does not predict qualities but very concrete things – with a certain aspect in the horoscope one will probably be bitten by a white dog.

Chinese astrology describes mainly long-term cycles, even though it also knows the division into 12 signs of the zodiac.

The original astrology, which originated in the early kingdoms in Mesopotamia, was a king astrology and and thus also a kingdom astrology. It derived the destinies on earth from the position of the planets in the sky. At that time it was still a collective astrology, which did not make birth charts, but only considered the current position of the planets, which had the same effect on all people. The kingdom was "the whole people" and the king as the connection of the people to the gods was in the world

7

view of that time the one through whom the effect of the planets on the earth came into the kingdom.

The astrology of the Mayas describes long-term cycles similar to the astrology of the Chinese.

The present book is about the occidental astrology.

II Occidental Astrology

The central element of this form of astrology is the horoscope. Such a horoscope can be compared to a play. Both have 7 elements:

1. One goes to the theater, the play has not yet begun, the curtain in front of the stage is still closed – the child has not yet been born.
Then the curtain opens and the first thing you see is the stage image – the sign of the zodiac in which the ascendant of the person in question is located.

2. Next appear the actors – these are the 10 planets, which are the same in every horoscope.

3. Each of these actors has a certain role, he acts in a certain style – this is the zodiac sign in which this planet is located.

4. Furthermore, each of these actors is assigned an area of life in which he acts – these are the 12 houses of the horoscope.

5. Now a script is needed. A script can ultimately be traced back to the relationships between the actors – these relationships are described by the angles between the planets. These angles are called "aspects" in astrology.

6. Now every play also has a director, who is responsible for the level of the play – this is the conscious ego of the person concerned, which is above the horoscope.
The "key" (i.e. the horoscope) of the soundtrack of this play is fixed, but whether you get to hear only weird sounds, or at least a simple children's song or even a symphony or an opera – that depends on the I, on the ego, on the director. This ego is the main creative source of the play – the ego coordinates and makes decisions.

7. It can also happen that the director simply doesn't know what to do with the script and is completely at a loss. Then he can turn to the script-writer – this is the soul that has decided on the incarnation in question. It will know why it has chosen this particular horoscope.

II 1. The Planets

In a horoscope play, ten actors appear: the ten planets. If they are arranged according to their apparent orbital period around the earth, a logical sequence results – on the one hand from the age of the actors and on the other hand from the development of their actions.

The **Moon** is a small child, which simply perceives and experiences everything and lives in direct contact with all things.

Mercury is a pupil who analyzes all these perceptions and examines them for regularities, discovering many a structure.

Venus is a youth who evaluates all the things that the Moon sees and all the structures that Mercury has recognized, and finds them either awesome or stupid.

The **Sun** is a king who makes decisions based on Venus' evaluations and sets the general direction.

Mars is a warrior who can act on the basis of the Sun's decisions and thus create facts.

Jupiter is a manager who takes the actions of Mars and directs them, combining them into a thriving whole and enjoying the fruits of his activity.

Saturn is a guardian, giving stability to what Jupiter has created, preserving and sustaining it.

Uranus is an inventor who sees the new beyond the known of Saturn and thus always initiates change.

Neptune is an artist and mystic who senses the big picture and through his longing creates the vision of a better world.

Pluto is a magician who grasps the essential and concentrates on it single-mindedly, thus bringing about transformations and performing miracles.

II 2. The Signs of the Zodiac

The signs of the zodiac result from the combination of the four elements (fire, water, air, earth) and the three dynamics (cardinal = creating, fix = shaping, mutable = using). In addition, the planets are assigned to them – as "kings" in the "zodiacal kingdoms", so to speak.

The signs of the zodiac				
	Fire *(deed)*	*Water* *(feeling)*	*Air* *(mind)*	*Earth* *(body)*
creating *(cardinal)*	Aries *(Mars)*	Cancer *(Moon)*	Libra *(Venus)*	Capricorn *(Saturn)*
shaping *(fix)*	Leo *(Sun)*	Scorpio *(Mars, Pluto)*	Aquarius *(Saturn, Uranus)*	Taurus *(Venus)*
using *(mutable)*	Sagittarius *(Jupiter)*	Pisces *(Jupiter, Neptune)*	Gemini *(Mercury)*	Virgo *(Mercury)*

The planets are distributed in the zodiak in a regular way. The three outer planets are added to the seven "classical planets" as "higher octaves".

The distribution of the planets in the zodiak			
Planets	*Zodiak*		
Sun/Moon	Leo (Sun)		Cancer (moon)
Mercury	Virgo (Mercury)		Gemini (Mercury)
Venus	Libra (Venus)		Taurus (Venus)
Mars	Skorpio (Mars + Pluto)		Aries (Mars)
Jupiter	Saggitarius (Jupiter		Pisces (Jupiter + Neptune)
Saturn	Capricorn (Saturn)		Aquarius (Saturn + Uranus)

11

Aries is a Taoist: He acts in the here and now – creating fire and the energy of Mars.

Taurus is an epicure: He gathers the pleasant and keeps the unpleasant away: shaping earth, which becomes harmonious through Venus.

Gemini is a curiosity seeker: He seeks the unknown and creates surprises itself – utilizing, moving air, in which Mercury delights in the colorful variety.

Cancer is a sensitive: He feels everything that is there and creates his intimate circle of relatives and friends – creating water filled with the security of the Moon.

Leo is an egocentric: He wants everything to go the way he wants, and is always at the center – creating fire radiating from the center of the Sun.

Virgo is a craftsman: She examines, repairs and heals all things and restores order – utilizing, moving earth imbued with the insights of Mercury.

Libra is a beau-spirit: He connects, arranges, balances, strives for harmony and all kinds of relationships – creating air filled with the beauty of Venus.

Scorpio is a concentrator: He intensifies, enhances, penetrates, fathoms all things – shaping water marked by the single-mindedness of Pluto and the power of Mars.

Sagittarius is an idealist: He searches for the optimum in every situation and strives to realize that optimum – utilizing, moving fire directed by Jupiter.

Capricorn is a realist: He strives for permanence and duration and creates solid foundations for this – creating earth, which receives strength through Saturn and becomes a rock.

Aquarius is a professor: He searches for the world formula and looks at everything from the point of view of generality – creating air, which receives realism through Saturn and is enriched with new ideas through Uranus.

Pisces is a dreamer: He traces and participates in everything that happens, and is like the captain of a sailing ship, using wind and currents – moving water that is grasped by the sensitivity of Neptune and used by the organizational talent of Jupiter.

II 3. The Houses

The houses, like the zodiac, are a division of the circle into 12 parts: The zodiac divides the year into 12 equal parts – the house system divides the day into 12 equal parts.

The ascendant is the beginning of the 1st house.

The **1st house**, whose area corresponds to the style of Aries, is the here and now. The planets in this house have an effect always and everywhere.

The **2nd house**, whose area corresponds to the style of Taurus, is the body, diet, clothing, apartment, house, garden, fields, and bank account. The planets in this house take care of the possessions.

The **3rd house**, whose area corresponds to the style of Gemini, is the new, the meeting, the learning, the conversations and the acquaintances. The planets in this house create new contacts and connections and do not like to do the same thing twice in the same way.

The **4th house**, whose area corresponds to the style of Cancer, is the family, the clan and the home. The planets in this house strive for security, shelter and intimacy.

The **5th house**, whose area corresponds to the style of Leo, is the throne room, where you receive your entourage and admirers. The planets in this house are concerned with self-expression.

The **6th house**, whose area corresponds to the style of Virgo, is the workshop, the doctor's office, the therapy center and the seminar room. The planets in this house strive for the healing state through insight, repairs and healing.

The **7th house**, whose area corresponds to the style of Libra, is the living room, where you meet the people with whom you are connected from the heart. The planets in this house are concerned with friendships and relationships.

The **8th house**, whose area corresponds to the style of Scorpio, is the battlefield, the police station, the brothel, the surgery, the yoga ashram, the magician's lodge and the cemetery. The planets in this house are always looking for what is most intense and for the place where transformations take place.

The **9th house**, whose area corresponds to the style of Sagittarius, is the tower from which one can look into the distance, it is the fire hall, the project office, the speaker's platform and the management center. The planets in this house strive to transfer every situation into the best possible condition.

The **10th house**, whose area corresponds to the style of Capricorn, is the office, the administration, the guard house, the federal border guard and the structural engineer's office. The planets in this house ensure that all important things are stable, resilient and reliable.

The **11th house**, whose area corresponds to the style of Aquarius, is the classroom, the lecture hall, the laboratory, the spaceship, the assembly hall and the clubhouse. The planets in this house want to change the world together with like-minded people.

The **12th house**, whose area corresponds to the style of the fish, is the hospital, the church, the street, the homeless shelter, the sailing ship and all the places where you can meet other people by chance. The planets in this house constantly scan all events and circumstances to see if one must avoid a thing or if one can take advantage of it.

II 4. The Aspects

The basic meanings of the seven aspects are quite simple:

0° = conjunction	= union
30° = semi-sextile	= developmental step
60° = sextile	= group formation
90° = square	= separation
120° = trine	= union
150° = quincunx	= transformation
180° = opposition	= swinging

In more detail the qualities of the astrological aspects are:

The **conjunction** has a distance of 0°. Two planets joined by a conjunction are like a marriage – they always appear together. The conjunction teaches one-pointedness.

The **semi-sextile** has a distance of 30°. Two planets joined by a semi-sextile are like a chance but momentous meeting – they are a developmental step. The semi-sextile teaches letting go of the old state.

The **sextile** has a distance of 60°. Two planets joined by a sextile are like meeting a good acquaintance – they can call on each other for help. The sextile teaches community.

The **square** has a distance of 90°. Two planets connected by a square are like a separation – they are like a tent pole that keeps the tarp above and the tarp below apart, creating a space. The square teaches freedom.

The **trine** is 120° degrees apart. Two planets joined by a trine are like a friendship – they help each other in all situations. The trine teaches reliability.

The **quincunx** has a distance of 150°. Two planets conjunct by a quincunx are like a constant buildup of order and tension – they challenge and encourage complete realism at every moment. The quincunx teaches love for the world.

The **opposition** is 180° apart. Two planets joined by an opposition are like two poles – they are a complementary opposition. The opposition teaches change in a constant swinging back and forth.

II 5.   The Ego

The ego is not an astrological element, but stands above the horoscope – it is not, however, independent of the horoscope. This I is the ability to be aware of oneself and one's momentary situation and therefore to decide consciously. This is shown in the small moment of pause between perception and reaction – this small moment makes it possible not only to react reflexively, but to decide consciously. The I is responsible for the level in which one lives one's own chart. This I is the director of the horoscope play.

This level question shapes the whole life: With a Pluto/Saturn square, is one may be petty criminal who either does only what he wants (Pluto) and does not care about laws (Saturn) or who is in jail (Saturn) and cannot do what he wants (Pluto) – or one may be social critic who contrasts one's own convictions (Pluto) with the status quo (Saturn) or one my be even a magician who overrides the laws of nature (Saturn) with his will (Pluto) …

The responsibility for the achieved level cannot be shifted to the horoscope – you are responsible for that all by yourself. The horoscope only gives the themes, but not the level.

Another important point in this context is that the horoscope describes the inclinations and desires as well as the abilities. This means that everyone has exactly those abilities that he needs to fulfill his wishes. It is therefore a matter of recognizing and understanding oneself as well as possible – then one will find out that what one is good at is also exactly what one needs to reach one's real goals.

II 6.   The Soul

One's soul has chosen for its present incarnation the horoscope that one has at the moment. The horoscope is therefore the style that the soul wants to have in this life. This means that the horoscope is not something that is imposed on you from the outside, but that the horoscope expresses exactly what you (i.e. your soul) want.

So you should not describe your own horoscope with sentences like "There is a problem …" or like "Fate has decided …", but with sentences like "I want …" or "I am …". When one comes into harmony with one's own soul, then one can realize that the horoscope describes exactly what one's own aspiration and fulfillment is.

However, it may take a while to get to this point, as one often mistakes fears, addictions, habits, cultural imprints, etc. for one's own true nature – which then leads to conflicts with one's horoscope. When you try to be someone you are not, it becomes difficult … and the more you affirm yourself, the easier life becomes.

III Individual and Collective Astrology

With the help of astrology it is possible to calculate and interpret the horoscopes of people, animals, companies, states and the like – astrology works constantly and on everything and not only on people. In addition, astrology can be used to describe the general quality of a moment.

III 1. One's Own Horoscope

The best known element of astrology is the horoscope. This is simply the position of the planets at the time of birth. With the help of the horoscope we can describe the style of a person, his inner structure, his preferences, his abilities, his appearance – but not the level at which the person lives all these things. The level must be developed by each person independently.

III 2. The Horoscope of Corporations

Horoscopes can be calculated not only for human beings, but also for animals, companies, states, inventions, marriages, beginnings of rulers and all other kinds of independent entities. The procedure is always the same: The position of the planets at the moment of independence ("birth") describes the character of what has become independent.

The moment of becoming independent can be many different things: the cutting of the umbilical cord, the word "yes", the signature on the registration of a company, the signatures on the founding document of a state, a coronation, etc.

III 3. The Horoscope of Other People

It is extremely helpful to look at other people's horoscopes as well, because this helps to see how different people are. Most of the time, this becomes really clear only after looking at a dozen horoscopes in detail. However, it can also become clear much later how much of what one believes "just is" is merely one's own subjective view and evaluation. Such realizations can lead to becoming more tolerant and to less misunderstandings, which are simply based on the fact that one has concluded from oneself to others.

III 4. Horoscope Comparisons

It is also possible to compare two horoscopes. This is done by looking at the aspects between the planets in the chart of one person and the planets in the chart of the other person. Since 20 planets are involved here and not only 10 as in the case of a single person (both have 10 planets in their horoscope), such a horoscope comparison looks quite complex at first. Therefore, one must first get used to keeping an overview.

By such a horoscope comparison you can describe the relationship between two people quite precisely. In most cases the two people can agree with this description, but the problems in the meeting between the two are not solved by this …

If the Mercury of one of them has a trine to the Mercury of the other, this means that these two people like to talk a lot to each other and can understand each other without much effort. If there is a square between the two Mercuries, on the other hand, there will be constant misunderstandings and ongoing power struggles for the supremacy of definition and for the definition of the frame of reference.

For example, if there is a square of one's Moon to the other's Mars, the person with the Moon will feel hurt by the other's actions and complain about a lack of empathy and closeness. The person with Mars, on the other hand, will feel constantly constrained in his actions by the other's attachment and sensitivity. In general, there is also a danger here that closeness (Moon) and sexuality (Mars) will collide.

III 5. Collective Astrology

Collective astrology is the oldest form of astrology. It starts from the observation of the current planetary position. The discovery that the planetary position at the time of birth or becoming independent has a lifelong effect happened much later.

The current planetary position, i.e. the relationships between the planets that can be seen in the sky on the given day, shape the events on that day. If you want to understand the current events, a look at the momentary horoscope can be quite helpful.

Once you have found the aspect in the current planetary position that has caused the events you are wondering about, you can also look to see how long that aspect will last – this will tell you when the situation will change again.

IV Predictions

In astrological predictions, individual predictions can also be distinguished from collective predictions. The individual predictions compare the birth chart or foundation horoscope with the planetary position at the time for which one wants to make a prediction – the collective predictions, on the other hand, consider only the planetary position at the time for which one wants to make a prediction.

IV 1. Transits in the Individual Horoscope

The predictions basically work very similar to the horoscope comparisons. One has the horoscope of the person concerned as a basis – the character described by the horoscope of a person does not change throughout his whole life, but this basic character gets different accentuations and colorings by the current planetary position.

For example, at the place where Mercury is in the horoscope, Mars can currently be up in the sky – e.g. both at 4° in Libra. This then means that Mercury, i.e. thinking and talking, receives the qualities of Mars, i.e. energy, as an aid. This leads to the fact that the things are formulated more sharply, that one becomes at times rather fast aggressive in one's speech, and one wants immediately to do what one has said etc..

If, on the other hand, Mercury is up in the sky where Mars is in the horoscope, the situation looks different. Then Mercury helps Mars to explain more precisely to others what one is about to do, or simply to find more clever ways to the intended goal.

These two examples are a Mercury/Mars conjunction. However, if the "running Mercury", i.e. the Mercury currently up in the sky, has a square to the horoscope Mars, for example, the person concerned will find it very difficult to put into words what he wants to do or to proceed according to a well thought-out concept. In case of a quincunx of Mars to Mercury in the horoscope, there are always new impulses to put into practice additional to what has been said, but the plans are constantly disturbed and stopped by something or other.

There are also some constellations that occur in all people. The best known of them is the so-called Saturn phase, which occurs at the age of about 28/29 years, then at 57/58 years and then again at 85/86 years. At these times the running Saturn stands again where it also stands in the birth chart – Saturn needs approx. 28.5 years for one orbit around the sun.

This constellation leads to the fact that one is confronted with what one has made out of his life so far. This also means that all deficits, fears, addictions etc. become conscious and stand massively in your way.

In this Saturn phase, for example, most soccer players have crises, don't score any more goals and change clubs after this phase, bands like Genesis or the Beatles break up when they can't stand the stress of this phase anymore and want to do something new etc..

The benefit of this phase is the possibility of a thorough self-reflection and reorientation. If one does not use this phase for this purpose, one will suffer from it more than anything else. Of course, the more old baggage one has in one's psyche and thus also in one's life, the more severe this phase will be.

IV 2. The Individual Annual Calendar

One can, if one wishes, create a personal yearly calendar, which shows roughly when one can do which things particularly gladly, well and consciously.

For this, one looks at which days the position of the planets in one's own horoscope corresponds to. For example, 16° Leo is August 8, 3° Capricorn is Christmas Eve, 13° Aquarius is February 4, etc.

On these days every year the Sun is on the planet in question in one's horoscope. For example, if Uranus is at 16° Leo in one's horoscope, the Sun will pass over Uranus on August 8 every year – this means that on this day one's intuition will become especially conscious and one will be able to put new ideas into practice.

Since this transition works not only on exactly this day, but also already 3 days before and also still 3 days after (and becomes first stronger and then again weaker), one has altogether for the 10 planets in each case 7 such days with an easily predictable quality – in sum 70 days with a certain quality.

One can also add the days on which the running Sun is in square, in opposition and in trine to one of the planets. Here, however, one should limit oneself to the day on which this aspect is exact, as well as the day before and the day after. While the conjunction and the opposition occur only once a year, two trines and also two squares occur every year.

So for each of the 10 planets you have $1 \cdot 7$ "conjunction days", $2 \cdot 3 = 6$ "trine days", $2 \cdot 3 = 6$ "square days" and $1 \cdot 3$ "opposition days" – making a total of $7 + 6 + 6 + 3 = 22$ astrologically relevant days for each planet. Thus 22 (transit-days per planet) $\cdot$ 10 (planets) = 220 days in a year have the same basic quality every year.

In this simple way a personal "perpetual astrological calendar" can be created.

Of you like you may also look for the sextiles, semi-sextiles and quincunxes but these are usually of lesser influence and not so easily dicernable. These aspects would add 3 (aspects) · 2 (two each year) · 3 (days) · 10 (planets) = 180 transit-days. Thus you would get 400 "day qualities" each year. There are obviously days without an astrological quality (direved in this way) and also days with more then only one astrological quality.

Of course, there are also the influences of the other running planets, but since these planets are located somewhere else in each year (since they do not need exactly one year for an orbit like the Sun), their influence must be recalculated for each year anew.

IV 3. Collective Events

Collective events are found where there is either no or at least no unified foundation horoscope. This is the case, for example, with the weather, but also with such events as earthquakes, tsunamis, or the outbreak of epidemics.

The easiest to predict astrologically is the weather, because there are decades of experience in this subject and the weather is based on manageable rules.

Since astrology always describes qualities, one must still translate these qualities with collective predictions into concrete events – this is not necessarily simple. This problem can be illustrated most simply by an example:

Pluto has been in a sextile with Neptune since about 1945 and will continue to do so until about 2039. This is the basis for all interpretations involving Pluto and Neptune during this period. This sextile leads to an emphasis on all things related to Neptune: art, magic, mysticism, social affairs, ecology, globalization, dissolution processes, drugs, etc. All these things are existential in these almost one hundred years.

In January 2020 Saturn has come to the place where Pluto is – at the end of Capricorn. This means that Pluto begins to shape the general forms of behavior (Saturn) – a collective theme emerges that concerns everyone.

At the end of February also Jupiter joined Pluto and Saturn – now the fixed, important forms of Saturn, which are experienced as existential and generally valid (Pluto), are organized (Jupiter). Thus firm and for all obligatory regulations arise.

In the middle of March Mars was added as a fourth planet in this conjunction and gave the triple conjunction of Pluto, Saturn and Jupiter also drive and a certain aggressiveness – this quadruple conjunction now enforces its principles with great emphasis and under threat of punishment.

Once a month, the Moon also completes this conjunction of four to a conjunction of five, when it passes at the end of Capricorn. All planets of this multiple conjunction have a sextile to Neptune. The gaze of temporarily five planets at the same place in the zodiac (Pluto, Saturn, Jupiter, Mars, Moon) is thus spellbound to Neptune.

In April Mars moves on, in May also Saturn – only Pluto and Jupiter remain in conjunction and the situation relaxes.

In July, however, Saturn returns to Pluto and the rules are again more strictly controlled and enforced.

Then, in December, this triple conjunction also dissolves. It can be seen that the situation will relax from then on.

This qualities of this process can be described astrologically quite easily – but how may one know that this dynamic will be based on a virus? The Corona virus is a typical Neptune theme (one of the negative kind), but it could also have been an environmental disaster, an art revolution, a new start of an effective climate conference, a migration or any other Neptune theme.

Once the theme has become visible, it is easy to see its further course with the help of astrology. However, to see the theme itself, in which an astrological constellation will show itself, requires skills beyond astrology.

IV 4. Long-lasting Aspects

There are some long-lasting aspects that shape whole epochs. These are primarily the aspects between Pluto and Neptune. This is due to the fact that Pluto does not have a circular orbit, but a very strongly elliptical orbit. This leads to the fact that it is close to the orbit of Neptune for about 100 years and consequently flies as fast as Neptune. After that, Pluto is much further away from the orbit of Neptune (further away from the sun) and thus flies much slower than Neptune for 150 years.

During these 100 years, the angle between Neptune and Pluto remains largely constant – both planets circle in the same velocity around the sun. If this angle corresponds to one of the astrological aspects, there will be a constant influence for 100 years, which all people born during this period will also have in their horoscope.

The chance that such an astrologically relevant angle occurs is about 1:4, which means that such a phase as the one we are currently living in (Pluto/Neptune sextile) occurs about once every 1250 years. However, there are much shorter variations of such Pluto/Neptune aspects, which may last only 10 years – they occur during both the 100 year periods and during the 150 year periods.

There are also similar aspects between Uranus and Pluto or between Uranus and Neptune. However, these aspects last only 1.5 to 2 years at the most.

All other aspects, that have a more permanent character e.g., those involving Saturn or Jupiter having a aspect to Pluto, Neptune, or Uranus, last a maximum of 1 year.

IV 5. Favorable Moments

If one can recognize the quality of a point in time with the help of astrology, it is natural to select "favorable points in time" for important projects. For this, one looks at which quality one needs: e.g. Mars for an argument – possibly also Jupiter, so that the whole thing has a chance to be constructive. If it is about a property, the 2nd house is important. So the running Mars and/or Jupiter up in the sky at a place which is in the 2nd house in your own horoscope would be favorable. In addition, Mars and Jupiter up in the sky should not have squares to the planets in your chart.

Which constellations are favorable also depends on your own style: If you want to solve a conflict by words, you need Mercury; if you simply want to defeat the other person, you need Mars and Pluto – and they may also have one or the other square; if you want to deceive and outsmart the other person, this is hardly possible without the help of Neptune and maybe some quincunxes; if you want to dissuade the other person from his plan with charm, Venus is the best helper and maybe a conjunction or a trine or a sextile …

So what is a favorable constellation in a subject depends very much on the personal style.

Then there is another fundamental problem: With the help of the choice of the time you cannot avoid already existing imprints – neither the imprints of your own character nor the imprints of other persons or the collective imprints. This leads to the fact that e.g. a couple living in joy and harmony can easily find a favorable time for their wedding and can also effortlessly carry out the wedding on this date – a quarreling couple, however, will only find a favorable time with difficulty and will then probably have to conclude the marriage on another day.

One cannot dissolve the already existing causes, circumstances and imprints by the choice of a favorable time …

IV 6. Time

One could now believe that the planets up in the sky guide the destinies of the people on earth. Since the course of the planets is already fixed, they cannot be directed by the people, but only the people can be directed by the planets.

However, at least two considerations speak against this view of things:

- On the one hand there is no force which could transfer this effect – the gravitation of the planets is too diffuse and likewise the electromagnetic force. The nuclear force ("color force") is limited to the inside of atomic nuclei. Also the telekinesis is extremely improbable, because how should the variety of the effects on the different people come about by it? The telekinesis is only an attraction or a repulsion, but it has not 10 different qualities like the planets.

- On the other hand, the character of a child is already shown in the womb – whether it is a calm child or wild child, whether it reacts to stroking of the belly or words and the like. Also the appearance is already pronounced at birth: long or short, thick or thin, the shape of the face, etc. All these things are already there before birth and do not arise only at birth. So the imprinting is already there when the birth itself makes the calculation of the birth chart possible.

So the planets do not imprint the newborn at the time of birth, but only the nature of the newborn becomes calculable through its birth. This means that the same processes take place in the child before and after its birth, which apparently also regulate the course of the planets. So the planets and the human beings are not in an imprinting relation to each other, but in a correspondence relation.

The horoscope is not based on a causal imprinting, but on an analogy. The world does not develop as a collection of independent individual parts, but as a whole, which follows certain rhythms and cycles, which can be recognized quite simply on the basis of the course of the planets.

From this it follows by the way that time is not simply a straight, steady flowing, as it is described in classical physics, but that each time has its completely own quality, which can be described with the help of astrology precisely.

Events then fit into this quality of time, so also all things that a person experiences.

V   Tools

When you have a horoscope in front of you or the current planetary position in the sky or any other astrological constellation, there are always planetary positions that you don't quite know how to interpret. Fortunately, there are some useful tools for such situations.

V 1.   Tarot and Horoscope

If you are familiar with the Tarot cards, you can place a Tarot card on each aspect of a chart or constellation to see what quality is present in that aspect. In this way you can also see which aspect is currently the cause of the difficulties because of which you are looking at this planetary position.

This method helps to get a first orientation.

V 2.   The Astrological Family Constellation

It is also possible to make a family constellation using one's own horoscope or another planetary constellation as a basis. The procedure is quite simple, but it will be necessary to have participated in a family constellation before to know what happens in it and how it feels.

First, place 10 sheets of paper with the planetary symbols painted on them in a circle on the floor in such a way that they correspond to the horoscope under consideration. The chart is placed with the ascendant pointing to the east, since the ascendant is the sign of the zodiac that has just risen above the horizon in the east at the time the chart refers to.

To place the planet slips correctly in the circle, it is best to place the horoscope in the center of the circle and turn it so that the ascendant points to the east – then it is quite easy to see from the horoscope where which planets must lie.

Now you can stand on the different planetary slips one after the other and see what you feel there, hear and see inwardly. Thereby one learns something about the present condition of the planets concerned.

Next, one stands on the aspects between these planets one after the other. In doing so, one will then learn something about the dynamics between the two planets in question – this is usually a bit more dramatic than the rather static experiences on the individual planetary slips.

Finally, you place yourself in the center of the circle – this is the place of the conscious self, which should be the director of the horoscope play. This is where you learn the most about yourself and about your attitude towards yourself and towards life in general.

These horoscope constellations are usually very revealing for the person concerned and often open up new possibilities of behavior for him.

V 3.   Dream Journeys to the Planets

Another possibility is to make a dream journey to the 10 planets in one's own horoscope or in the constellation under consideration. It is also possible to make a dream journey to the entire horoscope, but the dream journeys to the individual planets are usually clearer and more differentiated.

Such dream journeys can be made in a second step also with the aspects. Here it is the same as with the horoscope constellations: There is much more dynamism in the aspects than in the rather static planets – it is in the aspects that the real drama takes place.

V 4.   The Horoscope Assembly

Finally, one can expand the horoscope constellations and the dream journeys into a kind of horoscope ritual. To do this, one again places oneself in the center of the planetary circle as in the constellation and takes the role of the director – one is the conscious I in one's own psyche.

Then you can imagine a circular table (like the round table of King Arthur), where the 10 planets sit according to their position in the horoscope (like the 12 knights of Arthur).

Now you can start a conversation with the planets and e.g. simply ask how they are or if someone has a request, a complaint a wish or similar. Of course you can also call this planet meeting with a certain topic.

For example, if one has asked Mars how he is, one listens for the answer as in a family constellation or a dream journey, but one remains in the position of the director. Then one responds in an appropriate way to what Mars has said.

In these gatherings, it is like in gatherings of people: There are quarrels, misunderstandings, polemics, striving for dominance, resignation, etc. Therefore, a little experience with leading discussions in groups is quite beneficial – but not absolutely necessary.

The task of the director in these meetings is to keep his own goal in mind, to understand the concerns of the individual planets and to take them seriously, and finally to develop proposals (maybe together with the planets) that make it possible for everyone to pull together again instead of blocking each other.

Once you get a little practice with these chart meetings, they are an extremely helpful tool for understanding situations and problems and getting back on a proper, effortless and effective course that you can wholeheartedly agree with.

You may do this outwardly like in a family constellation or inwardly like in a dream journey.

As with just about everything, a little practice is beneficial.

V 5. Photos

There is also a general help in understanding astrology: Most people are able to recognize the character of most other people more or less precisely just by looking at their faces. Thus it may be a great help to collect pictures of people whose horoscope you know. In this way you may learn in a non-cognitive and more intuitive way the meaning of the astrological elements, i.e. of the zodiacal signs and the planets.

A comprehensive collection of astrological photos may be found in my book „Photo-Astrologie".

VI Development

You have your horoscope for a lifetime – nothing can be done about that. You can, however, change something in the way you deal with it …

VI 1. The Soul

Probably the most important point of all is that one's own soul has chosen the horoscope of its present incarnation. The horoscope is not a fate imposed from outside, but the expression of one's own will. About this view one can argue – and I know also some people, who hold a quite different opinion.

My view comes for the most part from my encounters with my soul in meditations, dream journeys and rituals, which have been going on for 40 years now, in which I experience it soul as my source. It is the entrepreneur – my psyche is the manager …

My psyche emerges from my soul's essence, my soul's intention for its current incarnation, my horoscope, which is the best possible style for my soul's intention, and my experiences with my own parents, siblings, relationships, culture, and so on. My soul is my identity – my psyche is the experience of the world through my soul.

This means that when you have recognized your own origin, i.e. your own soul, you can come into harmony with your own horoscope and not only affirm it, but experience it as exactly what you want.

VI 2. Horoscope and Chakras

One can think of the horoscope as a stone circle and the chakras as the world tree in the center of this stone circle. The circle represents the style – that is always the same; the tree represents the level – that can be varied a great deal (you may climb up this tree …).

If you do a lot of astrology for a long time, you see how all things are fixed in their rhythms and are inevitable – then you eventually become a fatalist.

If one practices a lot of chakra yoga and the like for a long time, one sees that all things can change and evolve – then one finally thinks that everything is possible.

But if you practice both, you can see that there are general rhythms, but they can be lived in different ways, i.e. with different levels – then an organic, down-to-earth development becomes possible.

VI 3. The Level

The level is ultimately the crucial point in all astrology: How do I deal with the position of the planets in my horoscope and the planets currently up in the sky?

To recognize and implement the possibilities connected with this is not an easy thing, because in order to do so one maybe has to dissolve old traumas, learn all kinds of methods such as dream journeys and family constellations, and above all find the courage to take steps into new territory.

VII Astrology and Magic

Astrology also plays a role in magic in several ways. However, astrological knowledge is by no means generally indispensable for working magic – but it is helpful ...

VII 1. The Favorable Moment

The problem of favorable times has already been considered in an earlier chapter. In magic, too, there is always the difficulty that one finds a favorable time, but for some reason one cannot perform the magic at that time or one is disturbed in performing it at that time.

The situation is somewhat different with the more general astrological points in time, such as the night of Jul (midwinter, beginning of Capricorn) or the beginning of spring (beginning of Aries). The four corner points of the year have the following meanings or qualities:

Beginning of Spring (approx. 3. 21.; Sun at 0° Aries; Equinox; Spring Festival/Easter): symbolism of the beginning or new beginning, of coming to light

Beginning of Summer (ca. 21. 6.; Sun at 0° Cancer; Midsummer; longest day): wedding, zenith, greatest strength, celebrating life

Beginning of Autumn (approx. 21. 9.; sun at 0° Libra; equinox; harvest festival): harvest, gathering, reflecting, ordering, caring, preparing

Beginning of Winter (ca. 21. 12.; sun at 0° Capricorn; midwinter, Jul; shortest day): birth (Christ-birth on Christmas), rebirth of the sun (the days are getting longer now), starting new projects (resolutions on New Year's Eve); Jul, Christmas and New Year's Eve were originally three aspects of the sun-birth festival

These four points in time, i.e. the beginning of the four cardinal signs of the zodiac, also play a major role in astrological weather forecasting: if a planet is at one of these four points and then has a square or opposition (i.e. that a second planet is also at one of these four points), the weather will be particularly severe.

The position of the sun in the different signs of the zodiac has a quality that is also clearly noticeable. If the months still corresponded to the signs of the zodiac as they did before the various medieval calendar corrections, these qualities would certainly be more noticeable than they are today.

Finally, there are the phases of the moon, of which the full moon is already visually the most impressive, but also has the greatest astrological effect: It builds up a tension that can be used to one's advantage if one acts decisively. Therefore, many rituals are performed on full moon. This is well known from sweat lodge ceremonies and Wiccan rituals. Easter is also oriented to the full moon: it takes place on the Sunday after the first full moon after the beginning of spring.

VII 2. Planets in Rituals

The planets play a much greater role in magic than astrology in general. The planets are regarded as deities and are invoked in rituals, asked to consecrate talismans, asked for help in healings, and so on. An important reason for this development from the last 150 years or so is certainly that the precise definition of the qualities of the planets gives them a technical flair, which suits the technically influenced zeitgeist of the last 150 years.

Also the cabbalistic tree of life, often used in magic, is connected with the planets.

VII 3. The Zodiac in Rituals

In contrast to the planets, the zodiacal signs play only a minor role in magic – although the 12-divided circle is the basic order in our world: as the zodiac in astrology, as the structure of the twelve-petaled heart chakra in Yoga, and in physics as the superstring, which is the smallest element of the superstring theory.

It would therefore be worthwhile to explore the meaning of the zodiac in magic. Since this division into twelve occurs when something comes into being and expands, it would be natural to investigate whether there is also such a 12-fold expansion, execution and realization in magic. However, this has not been done yet.

VII 4. Astrology and Mythology

The connection of astrology to mythology is rather loose. It is true that all along the planets have been associated by the people of Mesopotamia, Greece and the Roman Empire with their gods and have been taken as their visible image, but the qualities of the planets and the deities have diverged in the course of time, the more precisely astrology has been studied.

For example, in Mesopotamia Venus was once a goddess of war and not the goddess of love.

VII 5. The Astrological Description of One's Own Magic Style

With the help of astrology it is also possible to describe the way in which a person practices magic. Fundamental to this are the four outer planets, but the six others are also important. Basically, you do magic in the same way you do everything else in your life.

Pluto is the fundamental transformation – that is the core of magic.

Neptune is the extension of the limit of the range in which one can perceive and act – this is then telepathy (extended perception) and telekinesis (extended action).

Uranus is the sudden, unexpected, new – which is also an essential element of magic.

Saturn shows how to deal with limits and restrictions – and possibly go beyond them with the help of magic.

Jupiter shows what goals one has in magic and to what extent one is able to work with others in magic.

Mars shows how one uses one's power in magic and how warlike one is in magic.

The **Sun** shows what role one assigns to oneself in magic – in relation to the deities and the laws of nature and other people, for example.

Venus shows what style one likes, what things one desires and how one expresses that in magic.

Mercury shows the importance of words in magic, that is, whether one speaks and thinks a lot when casting spells or is more silent.

The **Moon** shows one's own handling of the life force and also the importance of security in one's own magical world view.

Of course, a person's ascendant is also of great importance for his or her style of magic, as are the planets in the 1st house.

VII 6. Healing

Finally, there is the use of astrology in healing. For example, the Ascendant shows which organ plays a major role in the person in question and is also the most likely to fall ill. These organ assignments are already very old and extremely reliable:

1st house (Aries)	- head
2nd house (Taurus)	- neck
3rd house (Gemini)	- arms, hands, joints
4th house (Cancer)	- lymph
5th house (Leo)	- heart, lungs
6th house (Virgo)	- digestion
7th house (Libra)	- kidneys
8th house (Scorpio)	- genitals, bladder, anus
9th house (Sagittarius)	- thighs
10th house (Capricorn)	- knees
11th house (Aquarius)	- shins, calves
12th house (Pisces)	- feet

The ascendantal zodiac sign shows which organ is most important. The planets in the astrological houses show which area of the body is emphasized by a planet.

Of course, the aspects also play a role – they show in which areas conflicts and, as a result, injuries and diseases may occur.

VIII   Subtleties

There are still a few "subtleties" in the interpretation of a horoscope or planetary constellation that are important because they allow a better understanding of astrology.

VIII 1.   The Signs of the Zodiac and the Aspects

The aspects can be derived from the zodiac and are therefore as fundamental qualities as the zodiac itself. This can be seen, among other things, in the fact that the zodiac and the angles of the aspects can be found with the same qualities in physics.

First group of aspects

VIII 1. a)   Conjunction

The conjunction is the 0°-angle, thus the identity – each sign of the zodiac is what it is … This angle, which holds everything together, corresponds in physics to gravitation, which pulls all matter and all energy towards each other. This is the simplest of all aspects: two planets standing side by side and form one unit.

The sign of the zodiac that is marked by the conjunction is Aries: live in the here and now, put all your eggs in one basket, be completely direct, act freshly …

VIII 1. b)   Opposition

The opposition is the 180° angle, that is, a "facing each other". This is the complementary opposition. This obviously corresponds to the zodiac sign Libra, which likes to combine different things and make a "we" out of the "I" and the "you". Because Aries corresponds to conjunction, one should also expect Libra, which is exactly opposite Aries, to correspond to opposition.

In general, all zodiac signs facing each other are opposition complements: the I of Aries and the Thou of Libra, the food intake of Taurus and the food excretion of

Scorpio, the diversity of Gemini and the goal alignment of Sagittarius, the inside of Cancer and the outside of Capricorn, the particular of Leo and the general of Aquarius, and finally, the detail of Virgo and the whole of Pisces.

This aspect corresponds in physics to the electromagnetic force, which has two poles: "+" and "−" or "south pole" and "north pole". This force causes a swinging and rocking and an alternation between two poles.

This dynamic of everlasting changes is described most extensively in the I Ging.

VIII 1. c) Trine

The trine is the 120° aspect; three trines make an equilateral triangle. Therefore, in physics, the trine corresponds to the three-polar color force, which holds the three quarks together in the protons and in the neutrons.

The trine connects qualities of the same kind, which appear in different forms. In astrology these similar qualities are the four elements: An equilateral triangle (thus three trines), connect in each case the three variants of an element – fire (Aries, Leo, Sagittarius), water (Cancer, Scorpio, Pisces), air (Libra, Aquarius, Gemini) and earth (Capricorn, Taurus, Virgo). A trine thus combines the three variations (cardinal, fix mutable) of a basic quality into one organic unit.

If you look from Aries to which zodiac sign a trine can lead, you will find Leo on the one hand and Sagittarius on the other. Leo and Sagittarius are the two trine signs, just as Aries is the conjunction sign and Libra is the opposition sign. Leo and Sagittarius are the two "organic signs".

VIII 1. d) Sextile

The sextile is, so to speak, half a trine – a 60° aspect. Starting from Aries, with the help of a sextile, we arrive at Gemini and Aquarius – two air signs. Gemini and Aquarius are the two sextile signs – Gemini playfully puts things together to form new combinations, Aquarius puts things together according to strict rules to form new combinations.

Air is the element related to fire. The aspects described so far combine the fire and air signs into a group of six signs: Aries – conjunction; Leo and Sagittarius – trine; Libra – opposition; Gemini and Aquarius – sextile. These four aspects thus give rise to a group consisting of the three representatives of each of two related elements (i.e. fire and air or water and earth).

35

A sextile always leads to a sign with a related element in the zodiac: from an air sign to a fire sign or from a fire sign to an air sign (respectively from an water sign to a earth sign or from a earth sign to an water sign). The sextile, that is, the 60° angle, is the principle of grouping as can be seen in snowflakes, honeycombs, the arrangement of spheres of the same size, and so on.

The same applies, of course, to the water and earth signs, which together also form such a sextile group.

Conjunction, opposition, trine and sextile form a group of aspects whose quality is the construction of a group. Consequently, there are four qualities in this group: the identity of the conjunction (each sign itself), the complement opposition (e.g.: fire and air), the conjunction of the trine (e.g.: three signs of the same element), and the relationship of the sextile (e.g.: fire and air). Thus, this group definitely has an inner dynamic, which is set in motion primarily by the opposition – however, this dynamic does not disturb the group, but makes it alive and gives it a pulse.

Second group of aspects

VIII 1. e) Square

The next three aspects have a different dynamic than the four that have already been described.

The aspect group that follows now consists of 2 squares, 2 quincunxes and 2 semi-sextiles, that is, 6 aspects. The previous group also consists of 6 aspects: 1 conjunction, 1 opposition, 2 trines, and 2 sextiles.

The aspect group just presented has described the structure within a zodiac group (fire/air or water/earth) and therefore contains conjunct aspect qualities (conjunction, opposition, trines, sextiles).

The aspect group that follows now represents the relationship between the two zodiac groups (fire/air and water/earth) and therefore contains distinguishing qualities (2 squares, 2 quincunxes, 2 semi-sextiles).

The square is a 90° aspect and has the quality of a tent pole: two things are separated to span a space. A square always leads to a sign of the other element group.

The two typical square signs can be found if you go from Aries 90° in the two directions of the zodiac. There you will find the water sign Cancer and the earth sign Capricorn. The spontaneity of Aries does not fit the introversion of Cancer nor the scrupulousness of Capricorn.

The same is true for all 12 possibilities of a square in the zodiac. There are always mutually exclusive orientations connected. Therefore, it is necessary for the two planets connected by a square to "leave each other alone".

This principle is demonstrated in physics, among other things, by the right angle (90°) that always exists between an electric wave and its corresponding magnetic wave e.h. in a photon (light): Both waves are separated from each other by a maximum angular distance.

VIII 1. f) Quincunx

The quincunx is the 150° angle. Starting from Aries, one arrives at the earth sign Virgo and at the water sign Scorpio by means of a quincunx. These are the two quincunx signs. They are characterized by the fact that they are never satisfied ... In Goethe's most famous drama it is about whether Faust can say sometime that he is satisfied or not – and Goethe was Virgo with Scorpio ascendant ...

Virgo wants to create order and Scorpio wants to create tension – these are the two sides of the quincunx. The quincunx always takes what is happening and then uses it to reshape the system that is already in place. Therefore, the quincunx is the "social aspect" that nurtures, nourishes, heals, seduces, provokes, transforms, etc.

Like the square, the quincunx always leads to a sign of the other element group (from fire/air to water/earth and vice versa). The two quincunxes, which can, starting from one sign, run clockwise and counterclockwise in the zodiac, always lead to two different elements, as in the square (and also in the still following half-sextile): from a fire sign to a water and an earth sign; from an air sign to a water and an earth sign; from a water sign to a fire and an air sign; and from an earth sign to a fire and an air sign.

VIII 1. g) Semi-sextile

The semi-sextile is a 30° aspect. It leads to the next or previous sign in the zodiac. From this its quality is already apparent: further development ...

Seen from Aries, it is Taurus, which reaps the fruits of Aries' deeds, and Pisces, whose sensing into the diversity of the world is the basis for Aries' spontaneous actions.

A semi-sextile, therefore, indicates that whatever one of the zodiacal signs achieves cannot last, but will evolve further on.

VIII 1. h)   Solo

Strictly speaking, the "solo" is not an aspect, but the absence of aspects. It happens in about every second horoscope that one of the ten planets has no aspects – so it stands alone and performs a "solo". This means that the quality of this planet cannot be directed by other planets, but only by the director, i.e. by the ego.

Therefore, with such solo planets there is the danger that they are not lived at all for a long time and at other times they are completely dominant. Therefore, with the solo planets, the vigilance and commitment of the director is needed even more than with the other aspects.

VIII 2.   Precise Aspects

Aspects that are very precise are a special case. We can generally say that aspects can be felt clearly when they deviate by a maximum of 3°, for example, when they are between 117° and 123° in a trine (120°). Up to 5° deviation is still just noticeable.

Now, however, in rare cases there are aspects which are very exact and have less than 1° deviation and therefore have a very strong effect within the horoscope. When such aspects deviate less than about 10' (60' = 1°), they begin to dominate the essence of the person or situation in question – ultimately everything then revolves around this one aspect. This aspect then describes the life theme of the person in question.

VIII 3.   The Two Sides of Aspects

When one has an aspect between two planets, there are five things at once that shape that aspect:

    1. the nature of the aspect,
    2. the two planets involved,
    3. the exactness of the aspect,
    4. the outer planet shapes the inner planet, and
    5. the direction of development within the zodiac.

1. The starting point is the type of aspect: conjunction, trine, square, etc. The quality of this aspect is the basis of the whole aspect interpretation.

2. Then, the two planets involved give this aspect two "colors" – the two planets are two notes, so to speak, which the aspect combines to form a chord.

3. The accuracy of the aspect shows how strong, important and formative this aspect is in the chart in question.

4. The fourth point derives from the fact that the sequence of the planets according to their apparent orbital period is also a quality sequence:

> the perception of the moment by the **Moon**,
> the analysis of the perceptions by **Mercury**,
> the evaluation of the analysis by **Venus**,
> the decisions of the **Sun** based on the evaluations,
> the actions of **Mars** based on the decisions,
> the construction of **Jupiter** by means of the actions,
> the consolidation of the constructions by **Saturn**,
> the addition of the new to the consolidated things by **Uranus**,
> the expansion of the whole by many new things by **Neptune**,
> the increase of the expansion to a transformation by **Pluto**.

From this sequence it follows that, for example, Pluto has a stronger effect on the Moon than the Moon has on Pluto: Pluto gives something existential to all the moods of the Moon. Of course, Pluto also receives the abilities to express itself in images by the Moon, but the general direction always remains the same: the basic beliefs of Pluto shape the moods of the Moon.

Ultimately, of course, each aspect is a reciprocal influence: thus, Pluto's basic beliefs naturally arise from the images that originate from the Moon's perceptions. However, when considering an aspect in the short term, the outer planet shapes the inner planet – the other direction only becomes clear when considering the longer term.

5. Finally, there is the fifth point, which depends on the direction of development in the zodiac. The deeds of Aries lead to the gathering of Taurus, then on to the curious experimentation of Gemini, then to the internalization of Cancer, then to the self-centering of Leo, to the careful elaboration of Virgo, to the harmonization of Libra, to Scorpio's search for the essential, to Sagittarius' orientation toward a goal, to Capricorn's consolidation of what has been achieved, to Aquarius' analysis of the

world, to Pisces' resonance with the whole, to Aries' spontaneous action, and so on. From this sequence a long story could be written effortlessly …

So the zodiac has a direction of rotation or flowing – the signs of the zodiac form a counterclockwise sequence. This means that a planet in Aries, for example, which is connected by a sextile with a planet in Gemini, is in the past in the zodiac sequence, while the planet in Gemini is in the future. The Aries planet forms the foundation and starting point for the planet in Gemini in this sextile. These two planets are like foundation and house, basement and second floor, root and crown, cause and effect …

So from the sequence of the two planets involved in an aspect in the zodiac something can be deduced about the character of this aspect. Thus, an aspect seen in the zodiacal direction (counterclockwise) has a somewhat different quality than seen against the zodiacal direction (clockwise):

in the direction of the zodiac (counterclockwise): further development, progress, crown, effect, construction, goal

against the direction of the zodiac (clockwise): recollection, search for support, reorientation, root, cause, safeguarding, origin

The seven different aspects and their two "directional qualities" are described in a little more detail below.

The **conjunction** has a distance of 0°. Two planets joined by a conjunction are like a marriage – they always appear together. The conjunction teaches unidirectionality.

Since the 0° angle of the conjunction leads back to itself, there is only one form of conjunction.

(For advanced students: However, in a conjunction, you can also consider the planet that comes first, seen counterclockwise, as the cause and the other planet as the effect – or the first planet as the "creator" and the second planet as the "further processor". The first of the two planets is the dominant partner in this marriage, so to speak).

Aries lives in the here and now, in oneness – this corresponds to the conjunction.

The planet that is called "planet 1" in the following aspect diagrams is the one that comes first in the zodiac – seen counterclockwise. „Planet 2" comes seceond in the zodiac.

40

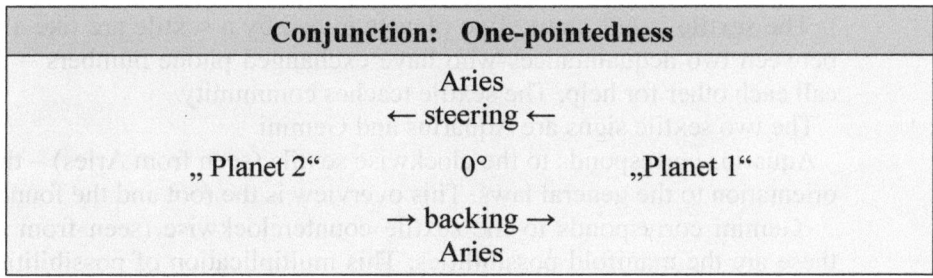

Conjunction: One-pointedness
Aries
← steering ←
„Planet 2" 0° „Planet 1"
→ backing →
Aries

The **semi-sextile** is 30° apart. Two planets joined by a semi-sextile are like a chance but meaningful meeting – they are a developmental step. The semi-sextile teaches letting go.

The two semi-sextile signs are Pisces and Taurus.

The Pisces corresponds to the clockwise semi-sextile (seen from Aries) – this is the intuitive return to the origin. This intuition is the root and foundation.

Taurus corresponds to the semi-sextile counterclockwise (seen from Aries) – this is the step into uncharted territory, taking in the pleasant and rejecting the unpleasant. This distinction is the crown and the fruit.

Together, these two qualities lead to reorientation by the semi-sextile. Pisces gives the semi-sextile the security of being able to find one's own way even in the unknown – Taurus provides the possibility of being able to seek out the pleasant and avoid the unpleasant. In this way, with the help of the semi-sextile, you can safely enter new territory and develop further.

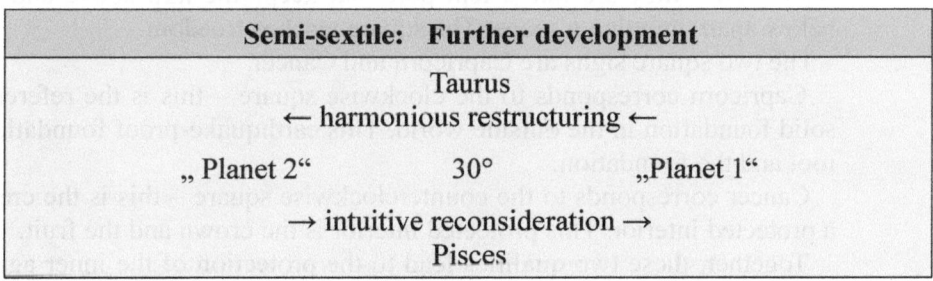

Semi-sextile: Further development
Taurus
← harmonious restructuring ←
„Planet 2" 30° „Planet 1"
→ intuitive reconsideration →
Pisces

The **sextile** is 60° apart. Two planets joined by a sextile are like a meeting between two acquaintances who have exchanged phone numbers – they can call each other for help. The sextile teaches community.

The two sextile signs are Aquarius and Gemini.

Aquarius corresponds to the clockwise sextile (seen from Aries) – this is the orientation to the general laws. This overview is the root and the foundation.

Gemini corresponds to the sextile counterclockwise (seen from Aries) – these are the manifold possibilities. This multiplication of possibilities is the crown and the fruit.

Together, these two qualities lead to group formation by the sextile. Aquarius sets the general group rules – Gemini curiously explores what can be done with these rules. In this way, by the sextile, you can create a group that is enriching for all members.

Sextile: Group Creation
Gemini ← multiplication of diversity ←
„Planet 2"   60°   „Planet 1"
→ common fundamental principle → Aquarius

The **square** is 90° apart. Two planets connected by a square are like a separation – they are like a tent pole that keeps the tarp above and the tarp below apart, creating a space. The square teaches freedom.

The two square signs are Capricorn and Cancer.

Capricorn corresponds to the clockwise square – this is the reference to a solid foundation in the outside world. This earthquake-proof foundation is the root and the foundation.

Cancer corresponds to the counterclockwise square – this is the creation of a protected interior. This protected interior is the crown and the fruit.

Together, these two qualities lead to the protection of the inner against the outer through the square. Capricorn provides a secure foothold in the world – Cancer provides a warm nest at home. In this way, by the square, you can create a space that is hard and cool on the outside and warm and soft on the inside.

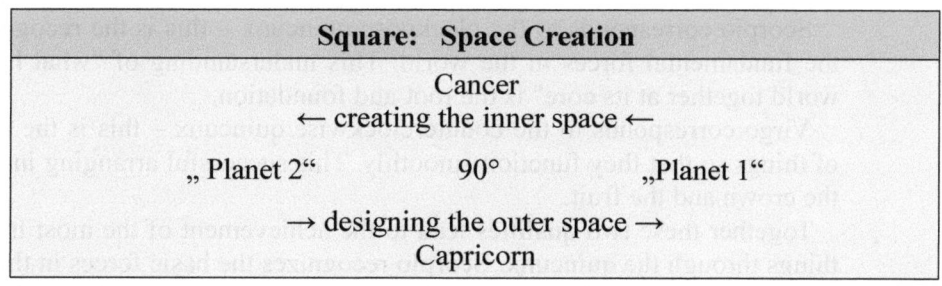

Square: Space Creation

Cancer

← creating the inner space ←

„ Planet 2"   90°   „Planet 1"

→ designing the outer space →

Capricorn

The **trine** is 120° apart. Two planets joined by a trine are like a friendship – they help each other in all situations. The trine teaches reliability.

The two trine signs are Sagittarius and Leo.

Sagittarius corresponds to the clockwise trine – this is the ideal that gives orientation in the world. This recognition of the best possible is the root and foundation.

Leo corresponds to the counterclockwise trine – this is the self-expression that is the goal in the world. This living out of one's center is the crown and the fruit.

Together, these two qualities lead to an organic lifestyle through the trine. Sagittarius enables one to see the best path – Leo has the power to then walk it confidently. In this way, you can let your personality shine through the trine.

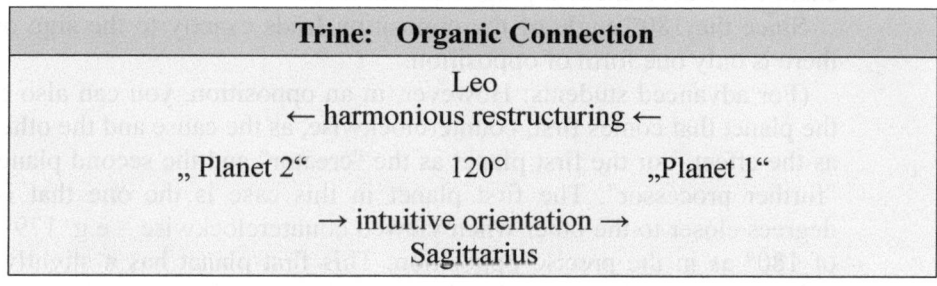

Trine: Organic Connection

Leo

← harmonious restructuring ←

„ Planet 2"   120°   „Planet 1"

→ intuitive orientation →

Sagittarius

The **quincunx** is 150° apart. Two planets joined by a quincunx are like a constant build-up of order and tension – they challenge and encourage perfect realism at every moment. The quincunx teaches love for the world.

The two quincunx signs are Scorpio and Virgo.

Scorpio corresponds to the clockwise quincunx – this is the recognition of the fundamental forces in the world. This understanding of "what holds the world together at its core" is the root and foundation.

Virgo corresponds to the counterclockwise quincunx – this is the ordering of things so that they function smoothly. This successful arranging in detail is the crown and the fruit.

Together these two qualities lead to the achievement of the most important things through the quincunx. Scorpio recognizes the basic forces in this world – Virgo creates the forms it needs. Together, by knowing the basic forces, they can create ever newer and more effective forms in their lives.

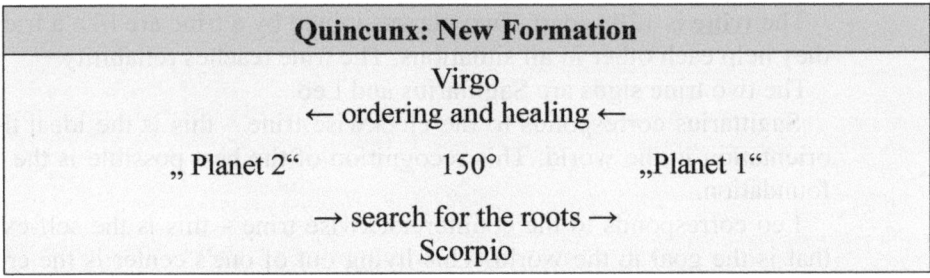

Quincunx: New Formation		
Virgo		
← ordering and healing ←		
„ Planet 2"	150°	„Planet 1"
→ search for the roots →		
Scorpio		

The **opposition** is 180° apart. Two planets joined by an opposition are like two poles – they are a complementary opposition. The opposition teaches change in a constant swinging back and forth.

Since the 180° angle of the opposition leads exactly to the sign opposite, there is only one form of opposition.

(For advanced students: However, in an opposition, you can also consider the planet that comes first, counterclockwise, as the cause and the other planet as the effect – or the first planet as the "creator" and the second planet as the "further processor". The first planet in this case is the one that is a few degrees closer to the other when viewed counterclockwise – e.g. 179° instead of 180° as in the precise opposition. This first planet has a slightly greater influence on the rhythm of the alternation between these two planets.

If Mars is at 10° Aries and Venus is at 12° Libra, then seen in the zodiacal direction (counterclockwise) from Mars to Venus is 182°, but from Venus to Mars is only 178°. Venus is therefore the 1st planet and the foundation, Mars on the other hand the 2nd planet and the advancement.

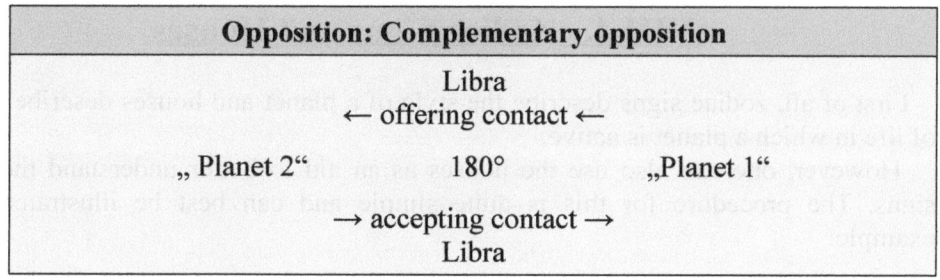

Opposition: Complementary opposition
Libra ← offering contact ← „ Planet 2"   180°   „Planet 1" → accepting contact → Libra

Overview: Zodiac Signs and Aspects

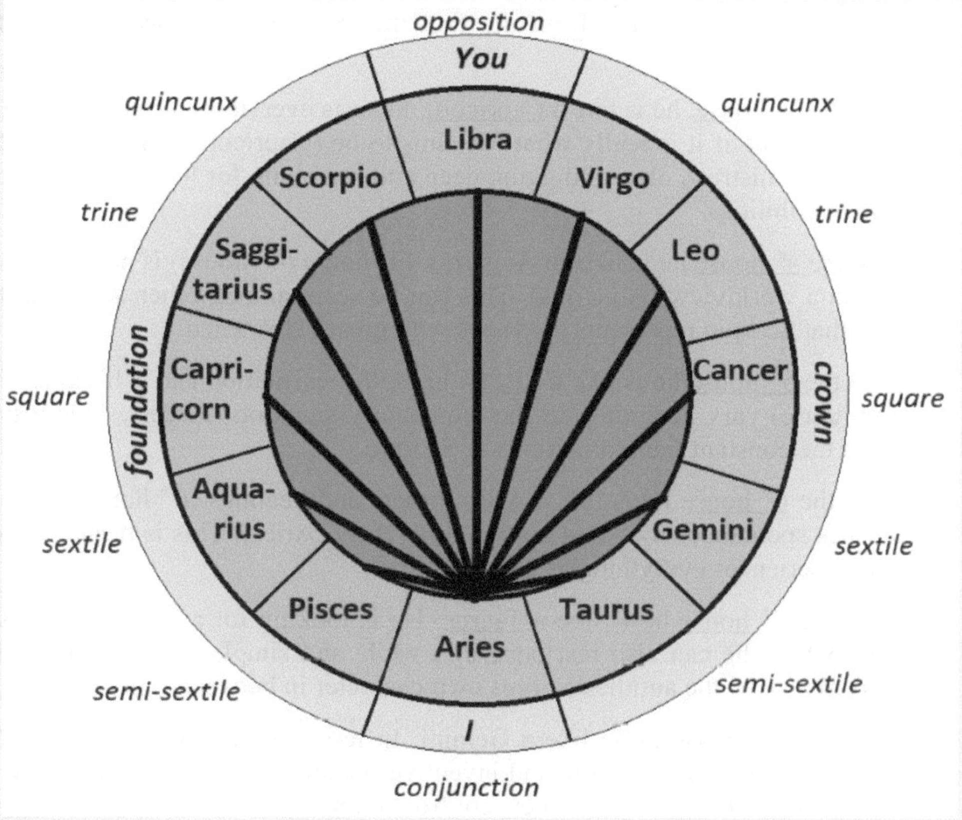

opposition

You

Libra

quincunx   *quincunx*

Scorpio   Virgo

trine   *trine*

Saggi-tarius   Leo

foundation   Capri-corn   Cancer   *crown*

square   *square*

Aqua-rius   Gemini

sextile   *sextile*

Pisces   Taurus

Aries

semi-sextile   *semi-sextile*

I

conjunction

VIII 4. Zodiac Signs and Houses

First of all, zodiac signs describe the style of a planet and houses describe the area of life in which a planet is active.

However, one can also use the houses as an aid to better understand the zodiac signs. The procedure for this is quite simple and can best be illustrated by an example:

In the 1st house, Scorpio behaves like a <u>Scorpio</u> – he feels, thinks, wants and acts "scorpionically" …

In the 2nd house, however, Scorpio is like a <u>Sagittarius</u>, the sign that follows Scorpio: He always wants to possess (2nd house) the best (Sagittarius) – he is an epicure. This results from the fact that Scorpio is always looking for intensity.

In the 3rd house, he is like a <u>Capricorn</u>: he tests everything he encounters (3rd house) to see if it is really what it claims to be (Capricorn). This stems from Scorpio's mistrust, always digging deep and searching for hidden motivations and possibilities.

In the 4th house he is like an <u>Aquarius</u>: his home (4th house) is not in a place, but in a worldview (Aquarius). This can be seen, among other things, in the fact that Scorpio represents his views with great vehemence.

In the 5th house he is like a <u>Pisces</u>: his self-presentation and self-expression (5th house) vary according to the momentary situation (Pisces). This results from the constant transformations of Scorpio.

In the 6th house he is like a <u>Aries</u>: orders and healings (6th house) he establishes spontaneously – and always differently (Aries). This is because Scorpio experiences everything as being in flux.

In the 7th house he is like a <u>Taurus</u>: He is looking for a "you" (7th house), with whom he can also rest once in a while and simply enjoy (Taurus). He may also need the antithesis of his own character in between times.

In the 8th house he is like a <u>Gemini</u>: In terms of strategy and tactics (8th house) Scorpio is very agile and inventive (Gemini). He also needs this to be able to assert himself in ever new confrontations.

In the 9th house he is like a <u>Cancer</u>: he always examines and re-examines (Cancer) what he actually wants and what his goals are (9th house). This is because he has no fixed self-image, but experiences himself as a process and as in a constant state of change.

In the 10th house he is like a lion: in public (10th house) he puts himself in the limelight and loudly asserts himself against all others (Leo). This is due to the fact that Scorpio is always convinced of how he sees things and usually considers this to be universally valid.

In the 11th house he is like a Virgo: world views (11th house) are examined very closely (Virgo) – and so are the members of the club of like-minded people of which he is a member. After all, he only wants to align himself with such views and surround himself with such people who are loyal to him and who support him in what he wants to achieve.

In the 12th house he is like a Libra: with all his distinctive contours, Scorpio is nevertheless compassionate and helpful (Libra) towards all people and living beings (12th house). This results from the fact that he experiences himself as a process in a continuum.

As you can see, you can break down the character of a zodiac sign into the 12 houses and then assign the sequence of zodiac signs to these houses. This then results in a differentiated description of the zodiac sign, through which one can discover one or two characteristics that one had previously overlooked.

The procedure is always the same. For example, Cancer in the 1st house is like a Cancer, in the 2nd house like a Leo (the sign following Cancer), in the 3rd house like a Virgo (the sign following Leo), and so on.

Only in the case of Aries, with its direct nature, the house always corresponds to the sign of the zodiac: He is in the 1st house like an Aries, in the 2nd house like a Taurus, in the 3rd house like a Gemini, etc.

The angular distance from the zodiac sign to the house always corresponds to the aspect belonging to that zodiac sign. In Aries, this is the conjunction: the 1st house corresponds to Aries, the 2nd house corresponds to Taurus, etc. In quincunx-imprinted Scorpio, this is the quincunx: in the 1st house (that corresponds to Aries) is Scorpio, which is 150° from Aries; in the 2nd house (that corresponds to Taurus) is Sagittarius, which is 150° from Taurus, etc.

It is not necessary to know these internal structures of the astrological system in order to interpret horoscopes, but their knowledge can help one to avoid the one-sidedness to which one will tend in the interpretation based on one's own horoscope.

All twelve zodiac-sign descriptions using this method may be found in my book "Astrologie".

VIII 5. The Aspect Structures

When looking at a horoscope, it is not enough to look only at the individual aspects, because it is the combination of several aspects into triangles, squares, rectangles, diamonds, and other even more complex shapes that reveal the basic dynamics in a horoscope.

A first step to get closer to this dynamic is to look in a horoscope which planets are connected with which ones. In most cases you will find 2 to 4 groups of connected planets. For example, Pluto, Sun, Mars and Jupiter could have aspects to each other, but no aspects to the other planets. Then, for example, Moon, Venus and Mercury could be linked by aspects and form a second group of planets. That would leave Uranus and Neptune, which could have an aspect to each other, and finally Saturn, which stands alone without aspects to the others.

Thus, there would be four aspect groups in this chart: 1. Pluto, Sun, Mars and Jupiter; 2. Moon, Venus and Mercury; 3. Uranus and Neptune; and 4. Saturn. Consequently, in the psyche of the subject there are four independent areas that can only be coordinated by the ego ("director").

Now one can look at the group dynamics in these four groups. In the case of the solo and the "duet" this is simple, but in the case of the group of three you already have two or three aspects which interact and result in a more complex dynamic.

For example, if the Moon and Mercury have an opposition to each other, one will be constantly switching back and forth between feeling (Moon) and thinking/speaking (Mercury). Then, if Venus has a trine to the Moon and a sextile to Mercury, for example, reflection on one's feelings (Venus) will always bring peace to the constant change of opposition, since Venus is connected to the Moon and Mercury by two conjunct aspects (trine, sextile). Venus is therefore the balancer in this aspect structure.

VIII 6. The Hidden Dissonances

There are some subtleties in the interpretation that are not immediately obvious. They arise from the fact that aspects do not have to be completely exact, e.g. a trine is not always exactly 120°, but may deviate by 5° – in the case of a trine this would be 115-125°.

A trine actually connects two zodiac signs with the same element, e.g. the two fire signs Aries and Leo. However, if one planet is at 28° Aries, an inaccurate trine of 124° ends at 2° in Virgo. This leads to the fact that two different elements are connected with a trine.

The trine still remains a trine, of course, but the "friendship" (trine) between the two planets involved is then a bit more difficult than usually, since different styles (elements) have to be integrated.

The same is true for the houses. Normally, a sextile links one planet to another planet two houses further on. However, since the houses can be of very different sizes, sometimes a sextile advances three or four houses or only one house. It even happens that a sextile is within a single house.

Close to the equator the houses are of the same size – close to the poles the differences in size between the houses are the greatest.

Deviations from the usual combination of zodiac signs by the aspects are rather rare: If you allow deviations of 5° e.g. from 120° (trine), you will find that 11% of the aspects link unusually signs (elements); if you allow only deviations of 3°, you will find that 4,5% of the aspects links unusually signs (elements).

There is however hardly a chart in which there are no aspects (if you are not borne on the equator) that do not link unusually signs (elements).

But this counts – as said – among the subtleties of astrology ...

VIII 7. Deversity

At the end of this chapter now follows a consideration of the diversity of the horoscopes.

There are 12 signs of the zodiac – this divides mankind into 12 groups.

Then there are 12 different ascendants – together with the signs that divides mankind into 12·12=144 groups.

Also the moon can be in 12 different signs of the zodiac – that already divides mankind into 1728 groups.

The same applies also to the other five classical planets, thus to Mercury, Venus, Mars, Jupiter and Saturn – that divides mankind then already into 430 million different groups.

Finally you can add Uranus, Neptune and Pluto, which again can be in 12 different zodiac signs each – that divides mankind into 743 billion groups. That's far more different horoscopes than there have been people since the dawn of mankind in the early Paleolithic.

If you consider now that a planet can stand at 30 different places in one sign of the zodiac (each sign has 30°) and thus completely different aspect structures result, you can assume that your own horoscope is unique – if not in the delivery room next door another child has been born at the same time ...

IX   Elements of Interpretation

A detailed description of all planetary positions in the signs of the zodiac and in the houses as well as of the aspects and the aspect structures would result in a rather thick book. However, since they are the basis of astrology, here follows a very brief summary of these possible combinations – this is only a first overview for beginners.

A basic principle in astrology is that no element can be interpreted alone. Of course, one must first interpret the ascendant and the ten planets individually, but the interpretation of the planets is always colored by the ascendant as well, since the ascendent describes the general approach. For example, Mercury in Virgo is always workmanlike and objective, but if the person has a Libra ascendant, he will always try to present his findings as easily understandable as possible for the other person, as well as aesthetically pleasing – after all, Libra seeks mutual understanding and harmony.

Then, when interpreting the aspects, the view of the whole becomes even more important, since no aspect stands alone, but is always part of the overall dynamics of the aspect structure in the chart of the person concerned.

Finally, it is also beneficial to present the different ways of living an aspect to the consulter – and above all, to make the person concerned understand the possibility of affirming their own style and raising the level of their own style more and more.

This overall view is something that develops only in the course of time by a lot of practice, that is, by the interpretation of many horoscopes.

IX 1. The Planets in the Signs of the Zodiac

The sign of the zodiac describes the style, role and character of a planet placed in that sign.

IX 1. a) Moon

Aries: One is spontaneous and fierce and direct, one's moods change constantly, one lives and experiences in the moment, one sees things sometimes this way and sometimes that way, one does not like half measures, even one's nightly dreams are short, simple and intense, one makes contacts quickly and breaks them off again quickly – a whirlwind.

Taurus: One is rather thoughtful, intent on preserving what is good and on keeping a distance from what is unpleasant, one collects and hoards and enjoys – a cook and a gardener.

Gemini: Moods are very mobile, one is curious and quick to react, one detests boredom and is enterprising, one sees (almost) everything, grasps things quickly, constantly has new ideas – a multifaceted joker.

Cancer: One is are sensitive, looks extensively at one's own inner life, is interested in the social sphere, the family is the most important thing, one has a rich inner life – a sensitive plant.

Leo: One always proceeds self-confidently, always has oneself and one's own needs in mind and asserts them, wants to be the center of attention – a lounge lizard.

Virgo: One is careful, cautious, always wants to get to know the circumstances first, examines the possibilities, is both knowledgeable and calculating, is easily irritated by trifles and easily delighted by trifles – a craftsman.

Libra: One seeks harmony, is balancing, conciliating and connecting, is oriented towards beauty and sympathy, is friendly, open-hearted, diplomatic – a charming beau.

Scorpio: One strives for the greatest possible intensity, always has the most important thing in view, looks behind the scenes, transforms oneself again and again, examines, researches, investigates, provokes, dominates and asks about the deepest roots of life – a deep spirit.

Sagittarius: With everything one sees, one also immediately sees what it could become, which is why one is always in a mood for departure, has several projects going on and is a bit restless – an active idealist.

Capricorn: One is businesslike, reality-oriented, slow, thorough, seeks out the greatest authority, creates solid foundations, builds on them, sticks to rules and uses all rules – a realist.

Aquarius: One floats above things and looks at them from above, has one's eyes fixed on the universal, appreciates being with like-minded people, founds associations – a professor.

Pisces: One is connected with everything, has a keen sense of all things, anticipates what will come next, achieves goals with a minimum of effort, feels part of the whole – the captain of a sailing ship.

IX 1. b)   Mercury

Aries: One thinks and speaks rather simply, one looks at the individual and the moment, one argues straightforwardly and directly, and one sometimes simplifys.

Taurus: One must know what thinking is good for, because why else should one think? The subject of thinking must be tangible, it must lead to an extended enjoyment – no thinking for thinking's sake.

Gemini: One can effortlessly grasp new views and contexts, one enjoys turning things upside down sometimes and then looking at them in a new way, one talks fast and lively and likes to play verbal ping-pong.

Cancer: One looks at things for a while before one says anything about them. Thinking is more like brooding over images than precise formulation. One says much less than one thinks. One is sensitive in conversation and either defends oneself fiercely or withdraws in case of dissonance. One always seeks contact with the other by language.

Leo: The vast majority of sentences begins with the word 'I', because thinking always starts from the I and leads to it. One understands things only if one relates them to oneself and to one's own experience.

Virgo: When the basics are clarified and the principles are defined, Virgo can logically grasp and present a matter step by step. The view is always directed to the detail and to the correctness of the argumentation.

Libra: One compares, weighs, connects, looks for the superior point of view from which harmony can be restored, understands both the one and the other, experiences oneself as part of the conversation and therefore has seemingly different opinions when talking to different people – one is you-centered in thinking and speaking.

Scorpio: One is critical, doubts, questions all things, looks for the motivations behind words, argues very strategically, is decidedly emotional in thinking and speaking, but usually hides this behind arguments that seem factual – an astute thinker and speaker.

Sagittarius: One always has the goal in mind, which is why thinking and talking is always a means to achieve a goal: perspectives, projects, goal-oriented argumentation, orientation, alignment, coalitions, etc.

Capricorn: The essential thing is objectivity – what one thinks and says should be correct and reliable and form a solid foundation. Therefore one examines for a long time, orients oneself to the greatest possible authority and thinks, learns and speaks rather slowly and thoughtfully.

Aquarius: One thinks in systems, according to principles and looks for the world formula. One looks at the world from above and wants to find the universal and formulate it conclusively.

Pisces: One thinks in hunches and speaks in hints; one orients oneself by impressions and comes to correct assessments and conclusions largely without visible logic.

IX 1. c) Venus

Aries: Feelings are spontaneous and fiery: today like this – tomorrow like that. They arise out of the moment and are true in the moment … and are in the next moment possibly already different again.

Taurus: The feelings are pleasurable and preserving; one tries to possess the pleasurable – even if these are people. One appreciates what is appealing and decorates what one likes.

Gemini: The feelings are mobile and always need the new – they want to explore how colorful the world is.

Cancer: The feelings are sensitive and introverted and ultimately seek a family in which one is secure.

Leo: The feelings are I-centered and one always goes the whole hog, one is fiery kind of romantic.

Virgo: The feelings are cautious and check first and secure – one is pleased by trifles and irritated by trifles.

Libra: The feelings are looking for harmony and beauty and one enjoys flirting and many contacts.

Scorpio: The feelings are fierce and conquering, they can provoke, seduce, put somebodys nose out of joint and are always intense.

Sagittarius: The feelings need a goal to blossom, but when this is present, there is no stopping you and you charge ahead.

Capricorn: Feelings are slow and steady, sometimes downright chronic – you seek lifelong security and dependability.

Aquarius: The feelings are abstract, i.e. one feels attracted by a principle – and all those who correspond to this principle, one finds beautiful and lovable and desirable.

Pisces: The feelings are diffuse, blurred; they come and go; they give orientation in

53

the sea of events and one swims along with the feelings and life.

IX 1. d) Sun

The Sun, for example, in Aries, is what is usually called "I am Aries." Although the Sun is only one of the ten planets in the chart, it is definitely an important one.

Aries: Decisions are made spontaneously and one sees oneself as a being that emerges anew in every moment.

Taurus: Decisions are made from the perspective of enjoyment and protection, and one sees oneself as a largely organic collection of different elements.

Gemini: Decisions are gladly made from the perspective of curiosity and one sees oneself as the red thread in a variety of experiences and encounters.

Cancer: Decisions are "brooded" over for a long time and one sees oneself as part of a family.

Leo: Decisions are made from the perspective of self-expression, self-actualization and self-expression and one wants to be the center of attention in every situation.

Virgo: Decisions are considered in all details and one sees oneself as a complex clockwork in which all parts are interlocked.

Libra: Decisions are made in relation to oneself and others so as to create the greatest harmony possible, and one sees oneself as someone who creates connections in the world between people and beauty in general.

Scorpio: Decisions are made in such a way as to achieve the greatest possible intensity, and one sees oneself as a being who seeks depth and is always transforming oneself.

Sagittarius: Decisions are always made in the direction of the best possible goal, and one sees oneself as a project manager and improver of the world.

Capricorn: Decisions are made according to the criteria of sustainability and permanence, and one sees oneself as an unchanging rock.

Aquarius: Decisions are made from a theory and a concept and one sees oneself as a member of a group of like-minded people.

Pisces: Decisions are made intuitively and one sees oneself as the captain of a sailing ship, using wind and current to reach one's destination.

IX 1. e) Mars

Aries: Action is spontaneous and direct and cannot suffer detours or complexities.

Taurus: Action is pleasure-oriented and only gets going when it is foreseeable that it will bear much fruit.

Gemini: Action is very agile and one does not like to do the same thing over and over again in the same way.

Cancer: Action is slow but steady, and comes in waves that gradually reach the goal.

Leo: Action is self-determined and needs the freedom to shape one's own course of action.

Virgo: Action is careful and considers all the details and sometimes makes complex plans for one's own course of action.

Libra: Action is oriented to the entire environment and, in order to maintain harmony, takes into account all the people and circumstances involved – effectiveness increases significantly in joint action.

Scorpio: Acting is like the classic drama: First nothing much happens, then it increases, then the transformation occurs and then it relaxes again.

Sagittarius: Action needs a goal in order to develop enthusiasm, power and effectiveness.

Capricorn: Action is slow, steady and oriented to all relevant rules and therefore reliable.

Aquarius: Action is oriented towards concepts and the world view and needs a utopia to really get going.

Pisces: Action follows the path of least resistance and thus reaches its goal with little effort on often strange paths.

IX 1. f) Jupiter

Aries: One always strives for new goals and cannot use five-year plans, but the spontaneous choice of the next goal.

Taurus: One strives for a sheltered place of enjoyment with abundant supplies of all good things.

Gemini: One strives for what looks most interesting at the moment and what is still unknown – just no boredom and monotony!

Cancer: One strives above all for an inner and if possible also an outer state of security.

Leo: One strives to express and represent oneself – the ultimate goal is self-awareness.

Virgo: One strives for carefully selected and planned goals, which one wants to realize with much expertise and skill.

Libra: One strives above all to create a relationship: the meeting of I and Thou is the highest value.

Scorpio: One always strives for new goals – depending on which goal promises the greatest pleasure and the greatest intensity at the moment.

Sagittarius: One always strives for the best – and when it is achieved, one needs a new, even better and higher goal.

Capricorn: One strives for what is most important to one in the long run and subordinates all other needs to it.

Aquarius: One strives for a form of universal living together, an association of like-minded people who strive for the same utopia.

Pisces: One strives for an attitude towards life that is only little bound to certain concrete external circumstances, but is rather a relationship to the whole world.

IX 1. g) Saturn

Aries: One finds one's footing in the moment and in present circumstances. One's life experiences are therefore individual memories which become conscious again in similar situations.

Taurus: One finds one's hold in the knowledge of what is good for one. The life experiences are therefore an orientation towards the pleasurable and beneficial – and in contrast to this, of course, also towards the harmful, that one strives to avoid.

Gemini: One finds one's hold in recognizing the variety of possibilities. Life experiences are therefore a collection of paths and their effects – as well as of all kinds of shortcuts, detours and interesting possibilities.

Cancer: One finds one's support and protection from the outside world in one's own inner being – in the image of the Great Mother. One's life experiences are therefore very subjective and pictorial, and focused on maintaining one's own security.

Leo: One finds one's support in one's self-image. Life experiences are therefore distinctly subjective and egocentric, but in contrast to Cancer, outwardly oriented.

Virgo: One finds one's footing in expertise and knowledge of details. Life experiences are therefore highly differentiated and varied, and ideally well ordered.

Libra: One finds one's footing in relationships and friendships and in recognizing the underlying beauty of everything. Life experiences are therefore on the one hand concretely related to individual people and on the other hand also generally related to encounter dynamics.

Scorpio: One finds one's footing in fixating on the most violent experiences – both the good and the terrible. One's life experiences are therefore a black and white picture shaped by the central and most intense experiences.

Sagittarius: One finds one's footing in the future, in one's projects and in goals. The experiences of life are therefore starting blocks for the future, for further action.

Capricorn: One finds one's hold in the factual observation and in reality, in the authorities of the area concerned. The life experiences are therefore a factual and dry foundation on which one builds everything in one's life.

Aquarius: One finds one's footing in the theory that explains the world – in the world formula. One's life experiences have therefore been transformed into a rather abstract description of the world, which gives one a general orientation.

Pisces: One finds one's footing in sensing the currents in the world. The life experiences are therefore very unspecific and are rather moods and hunches, which are nevertheless reliable.

IX 1. h)   Uranus

Aries: The unusual appears in the moment and is a creative idea – or a kick in the pants.

Taurus: The unusual recognizes new possibilities of enjoyment and thereby expands its own possessions.

Gemini: The unusual is a new possibility – actually it is usually many new possibilities.

Cancer: The unusual is a form of kinship that one has not noticed before.

Leo: The unusual is a change and broadening of one's self-image, a previously unknown aspect of one's identity.

Virgo: The unusual appears in detail, but enables great changes.

Libra: The unusual creates a new connection, a new harmony, a new form of beauty.

Scorpio: The unusual enables a new level of intensity and usually a transformation.

Sagittarius: The unusual is a new goal, a new project, and a new optimal state.

Capricorn: The unusual is a change in foundation or a change in formative authority.

Aquarius: The unusual is a new theory, a new world formula, or somewhat more modestly, a previously unappreciated fundamental principle.

Pisces: The unusual is a new current, a new wind, a new form of support.

IX 1. i) Neptune

Aries: Boundaries are spontaneously widened in the moment – the moment widens into world knowledge.

Taurus: Boundaries are widened by new forms of enjoyment – enjoyment expands to embrace the world.

Gemini: The boundaries are widened by new possibilities – the new possibilities widen into the great colorfulness of the world.

Cancer: The boundaries are widened by newly recognized kinships – the new kinships become a great intimacy of contact.

Leo: The boundaries are widened by self-knowledge – the self-knowledge is widened into the knowledge of the world as one great living being.

Virgo: The boundaries are widened in detail – the recognition of the new details opens the door to the realization of greater connections.

Libra: The boundaries are widened by new contacts and encounters – the encounter becomes a symbiosis.

Scorpio: The boundaries are widened by reaching a new depth and intensity – the intensity becomes the dance of life.

Sagittarius: The boundaries are widened by new goals – the new goals become a project of redeeming the world.

Capricorn: The boundaries are widened by new authorities and powers – the authority gradually becomes omnipotence.

Aquarius: The boundaries are widened by the recognition of new basic principles – these basic principles come together to form the world formula.

Pisces: The boundaries are widened by hunches – the diffuse hunches grow into a sure sense of what is to come.

IX 1. j) Pluto

Aries: The world is conceived as a succession of moments, all completely autonomous and at rest within themselves.

Taurus: The world is conceived as a substance to be kept, cherished and enjoyed.

Gemini: The world is understood as diversity, whose colorfulness is immeasurable and inexhaustible.

Cancer: The world is seen as inner life, as life force, in the center of which is the primordial trust in the Great Mother.

Leo: The world is seen as an all-encompassing individual – God is the consciousness of the world, which in turn is God's body.

<u>Virgo</u>: The world is seen as a great clockwork in which all parts work smoothly with all others.

<u>Libra</u>: The world is conceived as an all-encompassing harmony made up of complementary opposites.

<u>Scorpio</u>: The world is understood as endless struggle, ecstasy, transformations, and striving for ever greater intensity.

<u>Sagittarius</u>: The world is understood as something evolving towards a goal, which is why God is actually the future.

<u>Capricorn</u>: The world is conceived as a law to which everyone is subject and in which everyone can prosper only if he obeys this law.

<u>Aquarius</u>: The world is seen as a systematically structured entity and as the concretization of a fundamental principle.

<u>Pisces</u>: The world is experienced as eternal change, as an eternal flowing and swimming in which there are no fixed forms.

IX 2.   The planets in the houses

The 12 houses of the horoscope represent the spheres of action in which the planets appear in the life of the person concerned.

IX 2. a)   Moon

1st house: The moods, the need for closeness and the imagery of the Moon are involved in everything – the person is sensitive and in need of closeness.

2nd house: The Moon's moods, need for closeness and imagery work in the area of the body, food, housing, possessions and money – one needs a warm nest, has milk in the refrigerator and likes soft, cuddly clothes, provides for others or is provided for by others.

3rd house: The moods, the need for closeness and the imagery of the Moon work in the area of encounters and learning and teaching – one is sensitive, feels most comfortable in the midst of many people and is always open to new impressions.

4th house: The moods, the need for closeness and the imagery of the Moon work in the area of the subconscious, the family and the home – one seeks and creates security in the family and the home; one is the family type.

5th house: The moods, the need for closeness and the imagery of the Moon work in the area of self-expression and self-display – one experiences oneself in contact with other people, one expresses oneself by images and one cannot stand it when others want to change one's mood.

6th house: The moods, the need for closeness and the imagery of the Moon work in the area of ordering, caring and healing – one orders and heals by vitality and empathy.

7th house: The Moon's moods, need for closeness and imagery work in the area of friendships and relationships – one wants to cuddle with the "you" and experience security with him.

8th house: The moods, the need for closeness and the imagery of the Moon work in the area of intensity, research and ecstasy – one explores the inner images, pays attention to the facial expressions and gestures of others and strives for the intensity of contact.

9th house: The moods, the need for closeness and the imagery of the Moon work in the area of goals and projects – the future is designed as an image and contains above all the ideal of closeness, warmth and security.

10th house: The moods, the need for closeness and the imagery of the moon work in the public sphere – one makes sure that things are friendly and caring also in public contexts and is therefore engaged in social and charitable activities; closeness should be constant.

11th house: The moods, the need for closeness and the imagery of the moon work in the area of groups of like-minded people – one strives for security for all living beings and for the realization of the essence of the inner images, so that one can also grasp the original images underlying them.

12th house: The moods, the need for closeness and the imagery of the moon work in the encounter with the world as a whole – one seeks security in the world as a whole and the security that comes to one out of the world.

IX 2. b)   Mercury

1st house: The thinking and speaking of Mercury are involved in everything – the person understands everything very quickly and finds it difficult to remain silent.

2nd house: The thinking and speaking of Mercury work in the area of the body, food, home, possessions and money – one makes money with words, juggles possessions and eats all kinds of things.

3rd house: The thinking and speaking of Mercury work in the area of meetings and learning and teaching – one often talks to many people, likes to hear news and wants to experience something new every day.

4th house: The thinking and speaking of Mercury work in the area of the subconscious, family and home – you need familiarity to speak freely and openly, and you use language to make contacts.

5th House: The thinking and speaking of Mercury operate in the realm of self-expression and self-display – one experiences oneself most intensely in thinking and speaking; one speaks as one wills and does not allow oneself to be talked into it – the "I think, therefore I am" becomes "I am as I think."

6th house: The thinking and speaking of Mercury work in the realm of ordering, caring and healing – one appreciates the healing conversation and exchange with others by which things become ordered again.

7th house: The thinking and speaking of Mercury work in the area of friendships and relationships – one wants to talk to the "you" above all and to hear and exchange new ideas.

8th House: The thinking and speaking of Mercury work in the area of intensity, research and ecstasy – one is a researcher who questions all things and thus reaches deeper and deeper knowledge.

9th house: The thinking and speaking of Mercury work in the area of goals and projects – one likes to talk about one's goals and one directs every conversation towards the most ideal state that is possible and can be achieved.

10th house: The thinking and speaking of Mercury work in the public sphere – one likes to speak in public and also publish articles and books; one strives for well-founded and certain knowledge.

11th house: The thinking and speaking of Mercury work in the realm of groups of like-minded people – one thinks in terms of concepts and against the background of a worldview, as well as in terms of the utopia one aspires to.

12th house: The thinking and speaking of Mercury work in the encounter with the world as a whole – one thinks and speaks in hunches, assumptions and according to one's own intuition.

IX 2. c) Venus

1st house: The feelings and the sense of beauty of Venus have an effect on everything – the person concerned is an emotional and charming person.

2nd house: The feelings and the sense of beauty of Venus work in the field of the body, food, home, possessions and money – one decorates his body and possessions and earns his money through beauty and harmony.

3rd house: The feelings and sense of beauty of Venus work in the area of encounters and learning and teaching – one wants to create harmony in all encounters, flirts with almost everyone and spreads beauty.

4th house: The feelings and the sense of beauty of Venus work in the area of the subconscious, family and home – one creates closeness through a lot of charm, eroticism and beauty.

5th house: The feelings and the sense of beauty of Venus work in the area of self-expression and self-display – flirting is the elixir of life, the element in which one feels most alive, but also the creation of harmony and beauty are experienced as invigorating.

6th house: The feelings and sense of beauty of Venus work in the area of ordering, caring and healing – beauty is healing and flirting makes you healthy.

7th house: The feelings and sense of beauty of Venus work in the area of friendships and relationships – meeting a "you" is above all the search for eroticism, harmony and beauty.

8th house: The feelings and the sense of beauty of Venus work in the area of intensity, research and ecstasy – the beauty and the eroticism live out of an inner tension, out of the fire of the moment, out of the knowledge of the transitoriness of all things.

9th house: The feelings and the sense of beauty of Venus work in the field of goals and projects – one falls in love at first sight and always strives for the best.

10th house: The feelings and sense of beauty of Venus work in the public sphere – one works through charm and beauty and seeks lasting relationships.

11th house: The feelings and sense of beauty of Venus work in the realm of groups of like-minded people – one loves a principle and all who correspond to this principle one loves; one therefore tends towards polyamory.

12th house: The feelings and the sense of beauty of Venus operate in the encounter with the world as a whole – one is filled with a love of life and of the world as a whole, and one wishes to fill the world with beauty.

IX 2. d) Sun

1st house: The Sun's egocentricity and self-love are involved in everything – the person values all individuality highly and is clearly the center of his or her own life.

2nd house: The Sun's self-centeredness and self-love are active in the areas of the body, food, home, possessions and money – one wants to determine one's own appearance, clothing, etc., one needs a prestigious home and always wants to have enough money to be able to afford whatever floats your boat.

3rd house: The egocentricity and self-love of the Sun work in the area of encounters and learning and teaching – you experience yourself in the variety of encounters and make sure that you always remain the center of attention.

4th house: The egocentricity and self-love of the Sun work in the area of the subconscious, the family and the home – one wants to be the boss in the family and shape and direct it the way one wants it.

5th house: The Sun's egocentricity and self-love work in the area of self-expression and self-presentation – any criticism of oneself is almost an insult to one's majesty; one's own radiant self-expression is the highest value.

6th house: The Sun's egocentricity and self-love work in the realm of ordering, nurturing, and healing – any healing occurs through the restoration of one's identity.

7th house: The Sun's egocentricity and self-love work in the area of friendships and relationships – the contact with the „you" makes it possible to experience oneself much more intensely than one would be able to do alone.

8th house: The Sun's egocentricity and self-love work in the area of intensity, research and ecstasy – the ego is something that is constantly transformed and only blossoms in great intensity.

9th House: The Sun's egocentricity and self-love work in the realm of goals and projects – one has one's full potential unfoldment firmly in mind.

10th house: The Sun's egocentricity and self-love work in the public sphere – one sees oneself as a public person and is usually well known to many and strives for the desired reputation in the general public, i.e. for fame.

11th house: The Sun's egocentricity and self-love operate in the realm of groups of like-minded people – one sees oneself as a particular manifestation of a general principle; one tends to dominate the groups of like-minded people of which one is a member.

12th House: The egocentricity and self-love of the Sun operate in the encounter with the world as a whole – one sees oneself as a drop in the ocean and as a current in a river that is continually transforming and taking on new forms.

IX 2. e) Mars

1st house: The energy and eroticism of Mars are involved in everything – the person is energetic, combative and lust-oriented.

2nd house: The vigor and eroticism of Mars work in the area of the body, food, housing, possessions, and money – one likes to eat meat, wear sneakers, and fight for a living.

3rd house: The vigor and eroticism of Mars work in the area of encounters and learning and teaching – one feels most comfortable in a variety of activities, encounters and loves and does not like to do the same thing several times in a row.

4th house: The drive and eroticism of Mars work in the area of the subconscious, the family and the home – for drive and sexuality one needs a minimum of security and familiarity, but then it is reliable, considerate and helpful, as one works for the family.

5th house: The drive and eroticism of Mars work in the area of self-expression and self-display – one experiences oneself most intensely in sex and dance, in fighting and in sports.

6th house: The drive and eroticism of Mars work in the realm of ordering, nurturing, and healing – one learns martial techniques, the intricacies of the Kamasutra, the awakening of Kundalini, and believes that it is always a greater degree of power, sex, and dance that restores order or health.

7th House: The drive and eroticism of Mars work in the area of friendships and relationships – relationship is sex, work and struggle … and kundalini, ecstasy and tantra.

8th house: The drive and eroticism of Mars work in the area of intensity, research and ecstasy – one likes to seduce others with one's great charisma and one achieves one's goals with great tactical skill.

9th House: The drive and eroticism of Mars work in the realm of goals and projects – the amount of power at one's disposal grows with the size and persuasiveness of one's goals.

10th house: The vigor and eroticism of Mars work in the public sphere – one uses one's own strength to fight for the common good; one always does the job properly.

11th house: The vigor and eroticism of Mars work in the realm of groups of like-minded people – one can act and fight best in a group pursuing a common utopia.

12th house: The drive and eroticism of Mars work in the encounter with the world as a whole – one acts intuitively and takes the path of least resistance to one's goal, letting oneself be carried by wind and current.

IX 2. f) Jupiter

1st house: The goals and organizational talent of Jupiter are involved in everything – the person organizes his life and sometimes that of others and accumulates a great abundance.

2nd House: The goals and organizational talent of Jupiter work in the area of the body, food, housing, possessions, and money – one acquires an abundance of things: a "baroque belly," well-stocked pantries, ample living space, a well-filled bank account, other properties, inheritances, etc.

3rd house: The goals and organizational talent of Jupiter work in the area of meetings and learning and teaching – wherever you go, you quickly become an organizer and make connections between yourself and others as well as among others; you also recognize many possibilities and potentials and therefore stimulate many people.

4th house: The goals and organizational talent of Jupiter work in the area of the subconscious, the family and the home – one is the organizer in the family and holds almost all the reins.

5th house: The goals and organizational talent of Jupiter work in the area of self-expression and self-display – one's goals always strive for self-expression and one's own glory.

6th House: The goals and organizational talent of Jupiter work in the area of ordering, nurturing and healing – the reorganization of life leads to order and healing.

7th house: The goals and organizational talent of Jupiter work in the area of friendships and relationships – relationships and friendships consist primarily of organizing life together.

8th house: The goals and organizational talent of Jupiter work in the area of intensity, research and ecstasy – goals must be reviewed and reformulated again and again; one organizes the adherence to the principles – or sometimes the breaking of these principles.

9th house: The goals and the organizational talent of Jupiter work in the area of goals and projects – one organizes one's own development for the better and also the development of one's environment.

10th house: The goals and organizational talent of Jupiter work in the public sphere – one wants to build something that lasts.

11th house: The goals and organizational talent of Jupiter work in the area of groups of like-minded people – one is the almost indispensable organizer in the associations to which one belongs.

12th house: The goals and organizational talent of Jupiter work in the encounter with the world as a whole – one wants the best for the whole world and lets the world give the best to oneself as a gift.

IX 2. g) Saturn

1st house: The sense of reality and the wealth of experience of Saturn have an effect on everything – the person concerned always strives for permanence and is inflexible and holding.

2nd house: Saturn's sense of reality and wealth of experience are active in the areas of the body, nutrition, housing, possessions and money – one is frugal in consumption, gets by with little, but builds up a solid foundation in the course of one's life and one rarely changes one's place of residence, profession, clothing and eating habits.

3rd house: Saturn's sense of reality and wealth of experience work in the area of encounters and learning and teaching – one makes new contacts only when one has recognized their possible usefulness, but is afterwards reliable.

4th house: Saturn's sense of reality and wealth of experience work in the area of the subconscious, the family and the home – the preservation of the family is the highest value, since this is the support of the person concerned.

5th house: Saturn's sense of reality and wealth of experience work in the area of self-expression and self-display – one needs a foundation, training and a solid framework for self-expression and also creates such rules and solid forms oneself.

6th house: Saturn's sense of reality and wealth of experience work in the area of ordering, caring and healing – a clear order enables sorting and restoring the healed state.

7th house: Saturn's sense of reality and wealth of experience work in the area of friendships and relationships – relationships and friendships must above all be stable, reliable and predictable.

8th house: Saturn's sense of reality and wealth of experience work in the area of intensity, research, and ecstasy – one is a keeper of order and enforces one's views and guidelines with much vigor.

9th house: Saturn's sense of reality and wealth of experience work in the area of goals and projects – the optimal is achieved and secured by clear rules.

10th house: Saturn's sense of reality and wealth of experience work in the public sphere – one subordinates oneself to the general rules and at the same time wants to regulate the public sphere and ensure that these rules are observed by the general public.

11th house: Saturn's sense of reality and wealth of experience operate in the realm of groups of like-minded people – one upholds the groups of which one is a member and sees to it that what is necessary is done.

12th house: Saturn's sense of reality and wealth of experience work in the encounter with the world as a whole – one wants to give support to the world and receive support from it: a vision of detachment supported by responsibility for the whole and trust in the whole.

IX 2. h) Uranus

1st house: The wealth of ideas and the joy of novelty of Uranus are involved in everything – the person concerned is a little "crazy" and likes the sudden and unexpected.

2nd House: Uranus' inventiveness and enjoyment of novelty work in the area of the body, food, housing, possessions, and money – one likes to move, often tries new foods, has a wide variety of occupations, and sometimes wears flashy clothes.

3rd house: The wealth of ideas and the joy of novelty of Uranus work in the area of encounters and learning and teaching – the more exotic the encounter, the better; one always wants to experience something new and fears nothing so much as boredom.

4th house: The wealth of ideas and the joy in new things of Uranus work in the area of the subconscious, the family and the home – family and home change again and again, depending on where one can find the most security and intimacy at the moment.

5th house: The inventiveness and the joy of novelty of Uranus work in the area of self-expression and self-display – being oneself means being able to do any fancy and crazy things at any time.

6th house: The inventiveness and joy of novelty of Uranus work in the realm of ordering, nurturing and healing – to be healed, one needs something new, and to achieve good order, one needs new criteria for order.

7th house: The wealth of ideas and the joy of novelty of Uranus work in the area of friendships and relationships – one has a preference for "odd birds" in friendships and relationships.

8th house: The inventiveness and the pleasure in novelty of Uranus work in the area of intensity, research and ecstasy – one always finds a gap in what is allowed and moral and what is intended by others.

9th House: The inventiveness and joy of novelty of Uranus operate in the realm of goals and projects – goals are changeable and always new, and above all they are a departure into the unknown.

10th house: The wealth of ideas and the joy in new things of Uranus work in the public sphere – one finds new things, but is always careful that this is well founded and secured.

11th house: The wealth of ideas and the joy in novelty of Uranus work in the area of groups of like-minded people – the newer or more exotic the views and aspirations in an association are, the more comfortable one feels in it; one needs future-oriented utopias.

12th house: The wealth of ideas and the joy of novelty of Uranus work in the encounter with the world as a whole – intuition is a gift of the world and one also enriches the world by one's own ideas.

IX 2. i) Neptune

1st house: The art, the mysticism, the magic, the ecology and the social commitment of Neptune have an effect on everything – the person experiences himself as connected with the whole and acts out of the whole and for the whole.

2nd house: The art, mysticism, magic, ecology and social commitment of Neptune work in the area of the body, food, home, possessions and money – one likes to give, one likes to receive and sees possessions as flowing collective property, appreciates homeopathy for healing, has strange professions and likes spices and exotic foods.

3rd house: The art, mysticism, magic, ecology and social commitment of Neptune work in the area of encounters and learning and teaching – one feels into all encounters and helps, sees spiritual backgrounds, artistic possibilities and ecological necessities in all people.

4th house: The art, the mysticism, the magic, the ecology and the social commitment of Neptune work in the area of the subconscious, the family and the home – one merges with the family and does not believe to be able to live without it and experiences the feelings of others as if they were one's own feelings.

5th House: The art, mysticism, magic, ecology, and social engagement of Neptune operate in the realm of self-expression and self-display – self-expression is ultimately an endless artistic, social, spiritual, and oecological process.

6th House: The art, mysticism, magic, ecology, and social engagement of Neptune

68

work in the realm of ordering, nurturing, and healing – only the rediscovery of original intent, of fundamental order, allows for healing, which often involves a profound crisis and an equally profound transformation.

7th house: The art, the mysticism, the magic, the ecology and the social commitment of Neptune work in the area of friendships and relationships – in the encounter with the "you" the vastness of the world can best unfold; one needs a common spritual-social-artistic-ecological basis.

8th house: The art, the mysticism, the magic, the ecology and the social commitment of Neptune work in the field of intensity, research and ecstasy – one always expands the boundaries anew and thus experiences new territory of any kind.

9th house: The art, the mysticism, the magic, the ecology and the social commitment of Neptune work in the area of goals and projects – one strives for the ideal coexistence of all people, animals and plants, which is shaped from ecological, spiritual, social and artistic points of view.

10th house: The art, the mysticism, the magic, the ecology and the social commitment of Neptune work in the public sphere – one becomes a priest, a magician, an artist, an ecologist and is generally known in all these functions.

11th house: The art, mysticism, magic, ecology and social commitment of Neptune work in the realm of groups of like-minded people – one strives together with like-minded people for general peace and harmony.

12th house: The art, mysticism, magic, ecology and social commitment of Neptune work in the encounter with the world as a whole – one experiences oneself as part of the world and as connected with all living beings; life as a whole is what is actually real.

IX 2. j)   Pluto

1st house: The unity, the existential intensity and the conviction of Pluto are involved in everything – the person is therefore a transformer and constantly transforms himself, he always gets to the heart of everything and makes all things a little more intense than they would be without him.

2nd house: The unity, the existential intensity and the conviction of Pluto work in the area of the body, the nutrition, the dwelling, the possession and the money – one feels the own body as the most important, secures first the nutrition, protects itself against illnesses, needs a safe dwelling place and a reliable income.

3rd house: The unity, the existential intensity and the conviction of Pluto work in the area of encounters and learning and teaching – one is the formative figure in all groups and encounters and has an enormous circle of acquaintances.

4th house: The unity, the existential intensity and the conviction of Pluto work in the area of the subconscious, the family and the home – the security in the family and the mother are the central images and often they are raised to the archetype of the Great Mother.

5th house: The unity, the existential intensity and the conviction of Pluto work in the area of self-expression and self-display – there is nothing like self-expression, which is the essence of life and to which everything else is subordinated.

6th House: The oneness, existential intensity and conviction of Pluto work in the realm of ordering, nurturing and healing – healing and order is only attained by the rediscovery of the existential in a deep crisis and an equally deep transformation.

7th House: The oneness, existential intensity and conviction of Pluto work in the realm of friendships and relationships – the "you" is the center of life around which everything revolves.

8th house: The unity, the existential intensity and the conviction of Pluto work in the area of intensity, research and ecstasy – one searches and strives for "whatever holds the world together in its inmost folds" and also strongly shapes one's environment.

9th house: The unity, the existential intensity and the conviction of Pluto work in the area of goals and projects – the use of all one's strength for the goals is what makes life worth living.

10th house: The unity, the existential intensity and the conviction of Pluto work in the public sphere – the world is based on fixed laws and one seeks and uses these laws and thereby transforms the general public for the better.

11th house: The unity, the existential intensity and the conviction of Pluto work in the area of the groups of like-minded people – one is the revolutionary who inspires (or at least wants to inspire) the masses.

12th house: The unity, the existential intensity and the conviction of Pluto work in the encounter with the world as a whole – the actual, fundamental, important, original can only be grasped as a hunch, but its perception shapes one's entire behavior: it is what the Dakota Indians call the "Great Mystery".

IX 3. The aspects between the planets

The aspects in a horoscope are, so to speak, the chapters of the script of the "astrological play" in question. With 10 planets, there are 45 different combinations of 2 planets possible. Since there are 7 different aspects, there are consequently 315 different aspects in total. If one would describe these aspects all in detail, it would result in a quite thick book and not in an overview for beginners.

If you are looking for an aspect in the following chapter, you have to look under the inner, faster planet, for example "Venus", if you want to find an aspect between Venus and Mars.

Generally, the slower planet shapes the faster planet more than the other way around – the slower planet sets the frame, so to speak, in which the faster planet moves.
In a trine between Moon and Saturn, Saturn gives the Moon the wish that contacts be steady. The Moon also gives Saturn a greater empathy, but the permanence of the bond is still the much more striking phenomenon.
This uneven mutual imprint becomes more apparent the farther apart the two planets are in the planetary sequence. With a Pluto/Moon aspect, the difference in the imprinting intensity is greatest; with a Sun/Mars aspect, on the other hand, it is very small.
The planetary sequence is: Moon – Mercury – Venus – Sun – Mars – Jupiter – Saturn – Uranus – Neptune – Pluto.

There is a second such dynamic in aspects – it is based on the position of the two planets in the zodiac sequence. Since the zodiac develops counterclockwise, there is also a basic movement in the aspects that is counterclockwise. This is the order in which the Sun and planets also move through the zodiac.
This dynamic is most strongly felt in the semi-sextiles, which lead from one sign of the zodiac to the next. The planet that is in Aries, for example, is the starting point and foundation for the planet that is in Taurus, one sign further on. In this case, the planet in Aries is the past and the planet in Taurus is the future. So the semi-sextile indicates a progression from the planet in Aries to the planet in Taurus.
This dynamic is most weakly felt with the opposition, since in it both planets are opposite and therefore neither is the "first one in the zodiac".
In the case of conjunctions of several planets, this sequence helps to recognize the dynamics in this group of planets – it runs counterclockwise.

IX 3. a) Moon

Moon – Mercury

At a <u>conjunction</u>, one experiences no difference between the images and moods of the Moon and the words of Mercury – each image has a name and each word has an image associated with it. One is consequently very perceptive as well as pictorial in speech.

With an <u>opposition</u> one alternates between thinking and perceiving – both at the same time are not possible. It is important to find the right rhythm for this change between conversation and closeness.

With a <u>trine</u>, thinking comes to the aid of perceiving and sensing at all times – and one easily transforms any thought into an image or symbol.

In a <u>sextile</u>, word and image can also help each other, but must first decide to do so, while in a trine this happens automatically.

In a <u>square</u>, thought and image must remain separate – they are two different ways of encountering the world, and keeping them separate preserves their relaxation and clarity.

With a <u>quincunx</u>, there is a fundamental correspondence and basic tension between word and image, but it must be constantly restored. Every perception and every new thought must first be correctly grasped and inserted into the whole – but then it becomes an enrichment.

In a <u>semi-sextile</u>, both planets tend to move into each other's realm after a while. One cannot hold the image indefinitely, as it tends to transform into a concept – correspondingly, the concept tends to transform into an image. This transformation is mainly counterclockwise in the zodiac: for example, if the Moon is in Cancer and Mercury is in Leo, after a while every image and proximity becomes a word and a conversation. On the other hand, if Mercury is in Virgo and the Moon is in Libra, for example, after a while Mercury's concepts become the Moon's sensation and Mercury's conversation becomes the Moon's proximity.

Moon – Venus

In a <u>conjunction</u> one experiences no difference between the closeness and the images of the Moon and the feelings and the sense of beauty of Venus. One always wants to have closeness to everything beautiful and there are no feeling-free inner images.

In an <u>opposition</u> one switches rhythmically back and forth between image and feeling, between contact and evaluation. One is either in the experience of the situation or in the feeling – both complement each other, but do not take place simultaneously, but alternately. One makes mooneyes at somebody or embraces him – but not both at the same time.

In a trine, two closely related qualities enter into a friendship and support each other at all times: if Venus finds someone sympathetic, the Moon also wants to hug them; if Venus has a feeling, the Moon also has a picture of it.

In a sextile, two planets in zodiac signs with different but similar qualities occasionally support each other: outer contacts and inner images are usually, but not always, connected with feelings.

With a square, you always check which of the two qualities you want to use – and the other quality stays out of it completely: either you have contact or you have a feeling, but not both at the same time. This makes the feelings seem a little distant and the contacts a little cool.

In a quincunx, closeness and feeling constantly restore order and tension. Feelings are easily irritated, which leads to a withdrawal – after clarification, however, closeness occurs again. Or the feelings subside, whereupon a consideration of the causes leads to a renewed blossoming of feelings.

In a semi-sextile, either the closeness or the feelings push for further development. Thus closeness becomes feeling, causing closeness to lessen – or feeling becomes contact, causing feelings to partially fade.

Moon – Sun

In a conjunction, one experiences no difference between the images and perceptions of the Moon and one's own center: One is inseparable from one's own perceptions, images and contacts – one is one's own family.

In an opposition one alternates rhythmically back and forth between image and center, between contact and identity. One sees alternately oneself and the others – and does not mix the two.

In a trine, two closely related qualities enter into a friendship and support each other at all times: the heart (Sun) seeks contact (Moon) and the contact is filled with individual warmth – closeness becomes self-expression.

In a sextile, two planets in zodiac signs with different but similar qualities occasionally support each other: moods have the opportunity to become conscious, and the ego has the opportunity to make contact.

With a square, one is always checking anew in every situation which of the two qualities one wants to use – and the other quality stays completely out of it: sensation or self-expression, image or self-image, community or egoism.

In a quincunx, sensibility and self-expression are always re-establishing order and tension. This leads to constant self-questioning and frequent renewal of contacts.

In a <u>semi-sextile</u>, either contact or self-esteem urges further development, which then leads to the other. As a result, either closeness becomes more cordial (Moon => Sun) or new contact emerges from freer self-expression (Sun => Moon).

Moon – Mars

In a <u>conjunction</u> one experiences no difference between closeness and action. One experiences the greatest closeness in sex, work and struggle – action without contact is hardly possible; an inner image that does not urge action is hardly conceivable.

In an <u>opposition</u>, one alternates rhythmically back and forth between image and deed, between contact and action. One broods over what is important to one, and then proceeds to action, and afterwards one contemplates again in silence what has been done. One lives alternately the intimacy of closeness and the ecstasy of sex.

In a <u>trine</u>, two closely related qualities enter into a friendship and support each other at all times: one acts in awareness of one's surroundings and with contact to them. Closeness/security and sex/action enter into a friendship and are always connected.

In a <u>sextile</u>, two planets in zodiac signs with different but similar qualities occasionally support each other: sensations have the possibility of becoming deeds, and deeds have the possibility of being sensitive.

In a <u>square</u>, one always reassesses which of the two qualities one wants to use in a given situation – and the other quality stays out of it completely: Proximity or sex, contact or detachment, perception or deed.

In a <u>quincunx</u>, closeness and action always re-establish order and tension. Among other things, this leads to frequent questioning and possibly renewal of the form of the relationship in terms of closeness and sexuality.

With a <u>semi-sextile</u> either sensitivities or desires push for a further development – thus e.g. closeness changes into sex or sex into closeness after a while.

Moon – Jupiter

With a <u>conjunction</u> one experiences no difference between contacts and management: one organizes one's contacts and joins them to a community. One also never sees inner images individually, but always as part of a larger structure.

In an <u>opposition</u>, one switches rhythmically back and forth between image and goals, between contact and organization. One is sometimes the manager and sometimes the observer, one sometimes reaches out to the others and sometimes one directs them.

In a trine, two closely related qualities enter into a friendship and support each other at all times: one organizes all connections with people and creates from this a community in which everyone feels comfortable.

In a sextile, two planets in zodiac signs with different but similar qualities occasionally support each other: contacts have the possibility of becoming part of the fabric of relationships, and one's organizing has the possibility of creating a large nest for all the people one cares about.

With a square, one is always re-evaluating which of the two qualities one wants to use in a given situation – and the other quality stays out of it completely: contact or organization, closeness or goals, community or ideals.

In a quincunx, closeness and life design always re-establish the order and the tension. This leads to ever new revisions of relationships and how the various relationships relate to each other, as well as new views of relationships and family as a whole from time to time.

In a semi-sextile, either the closeness or the organization of life urges a further development towards the other, whereby either the closeness subsides and becomes pure organization, or the organizing subsides and becomes closeness – it depends on which of the two planets comes first in the sequence of the zodiacal signs.

Moon – Saturn

With a conjunction one experiences no difference between contact and permanence: contacts are always permanent. In addition, one's own foundation is grasped pictorially, rules must be felt, there is support only in the encounter …

In an opposition one switches rhythmically back and forth between image and form, between contact and foundation. One cares sometimes that everything is stable and reliable and permanent, and then again that one is in contact with everyone. One alternates between "letting things go well" and "making sure that everything is settled".

In a trine, two closely related qualities form a friendship and support each other at all times: contacts are always constant and every form is to create well-being and comfort.

In a sextile, two planets in zodiac signs with different but similar qualities occasionally support each other: contacts have the possibility of becoming secure and stable, and the forms in one's life have the possibility of becoming a protection for one's contacts.

With a square, one always reassesses which of the two qualities one wants to use in a given situation – and the other quality stays out of it completely: Closeness or constancy, contact or form, image or law.

In a quincunx, closeness and form always re-establish order and tension. This leads again and again to new insights, preferences, views and changes in the previous arrangements – ever moving contacts …

In a semi-sextile either the closeness or the formal determination pushes for a further development to the respective other quality. As a result, either the closeness becomes more formal (Moon => Saturn) or a new contact emerges from an external form (Saturn => Moon).

Moon – Uranus

In a conjunction one experiences no difference between the inner images and intuition: one makes contact spontaneously; one experiences things as more vivid when they are new; moods change constantly and suddenly; one grasps new things very quickly …

In an opposition, one switches rhythmically back and forth between image and intuition, between contact and the new. One changes from being close to bouncing around and then back to being close again – in a rather unpredictable rhythm.

In a trine, two closely related qualities enter into a friendship and support each other at all times: contacts are made quickly and sometimes are also ended quickly. One lives closeness in the moment of experience.

In a sextile, two planets in zodiac signs with different but similar qualities occasionally support each other: moods have the possibility to be spontaneous and intuition has the possibility to make contacts.

With a square, one always reassesses which of the two qualities one wants to use in a given situation – and the other quality stays out of it completely: sentiment or intuition, closeness or newness, holding or jumping.

In a quincunx, closeness and spontaneity always re-establish order and tension. This leads to the necessity to sit down again and again and to see if and if so, how the previous relationship can still be continued with the new impulses.

In a semi-sextile, either closeness or spontaneity pushes for a further development to the respective other quality. This will either suddenly change the closeness (Moon => Uranus) or suddenly create a new contact (Uranus => Moon).

Moon – Neptune

In a conjunction one experiences no difference between the image and the archetype. Neptune dissolves the boundaries of the inner images so that they become part of the general images; perception becomes telepathy; the individual subconscious becomes the collective subconscious; contact becomes symbiosis …

76

In an opposition, one switches rhythmically back and forth between image and fantasy, between contact and symbiosis. Both create closeness, but the Moon to the individual and the Neptune to the world. Therefore, one alternates back and forth between alignment with the "you" and alignment with the world – this can be like a breathing rhythm.

In a trine, two closely related qualities enter into a friendship and support each other at all times: closeness becomes symbiosis, images become archetypes, and understanding becomes telepathy.

With a sextile, two planets in zodiac signs with different but similar qualities occasionally support each other: proximity has the possibility of increasing to symbiosis and effortless telepathy, and boundary dissolution has the possibility of becoming a broad sense of family and home.

With a square one always checks anew in every situation which of the two qualities one wants to use – and the other quality stays completely out of it: image or archetype, security in the concrete or security in the general, warmth or art, holding hands or meditate.

In a quincunx, closeness and boundary dissolution establish the order and the tension again and again. This leads to the question of where to set boundaries in proximity and where not – and how to dissolve existing boundaries … and how to deal with the constant dissolving and reshaping of encounters in general. The question of how to reconcile proximity with art, religion and ecology also arises again and again.

In a semi-sextile, either proximity or boundary dissolution urge a progression to the other quality. Thereby either the closeness is extended (Moon => Neptune) or a new contact arises out of art, social commitment, ecology or religion (Neptune => Moon).

Moon – Pluto

In a conjunction, one experiences no difference between contact and the existential – contact is always essential and existential. Contact is what life is all about – and one never does things half-heartedly …

In an opposition one switches rhythmically back and forth between image and essential, between contact and essential. Sometimes one is completely in one's own conviction and follows this unswervingly – then one is again completely in contact and perceives the outside. One is alternately like the moonlight and like a laser beam.

In a trine, two closely related qualities enter into friendship and support each other at all times: closeness is the elixir of life, contact is existential, security is the root, the archetype of all things is the Great Mother.

In a sextile, two planets in zodiac signs with different but similar qualities occasionally support each other: moods have the possibility to become intense, and the essential has the possibility to be experienced as an image.

In a square, one always checks anew in a given situation which of the two qualities one wants to use – and the other quality stays out of it completely: perception or conviction, contact or essence, proximity or essential.

In a quincunx, closeness and essence always re-establish order and tension. As a result, one often wonders if one even wants a relationship anymore, and if an encounter can still be reconciled with what's really important to oneself.

In a semi-sextile, either closeness or basic beliefs urge a progression to the other quality. Thus either the closeness becomes very intense (Moon => Pluto) or a new contact arises out of profound transformations (Pluto => Moon).

IX 3. b) Mercury

Mercury – Venus

In a conjunction one experiences no difference between thinking and feeling: Every thought also contains an evaluation and every evaluation is also put into words. The language is charming and emotional and moving.

The opposition, trine, square and quincunx are not possible between the Sun and Mercury because the maximum distance between the two as seen from Earth (as they appear in the chart) is 72° – so only the conjunction (0°), the semi-sextile (30°) and the sextile (60°) are possible. The 72° result from the 27° maximum distance of Mercury from the Sun and the 45° maximum distance of Venus from the Sun.

In a sextile, two planets in zodiac signs with different but similar characteristics occasionally support each other: thoughts have the possibility of becoming feelings, and feelings have the possibility of being expressed by words.

In a semi-sextile, either mind or feeling urges progression to the other quality. As a result, either the mind becomes emotional (Mercury => Venus) or the feelings become rational (Venus => Mercury).

Mercury – Sun

With a conjunction, one experiences no difference between ego and thinking: thinking is an expression of the ego; one's own ego is always the center of thinking; sentences usually begin with "I"; one relates all words to oneself …

The opposition, the trine, the sextile, the square and the quincunx are not possible between Sun and Mercury, because the maximum distance between them seen from Earth (as they appear in the chart) is 27° – so only the conjunction (0°) and an inaccurate semi-sextile (30°) are possible.

With a semi-sextile, either mind or self-expression pushes for progression to the other quality. As a result, either the mind becomes egocentric (Mercury => Sun) or self-expression becomes rational (Sun => Mercury).

Mercury – Mars

With a conjunction, one experiences no difference between word and deed: one does what one says; one talks while doing; one has a concept about one's actions; one can change direction in action at any time if it seems more sensible … "A mans word is his bond."

In an opposition, one switches rhythmically back and forth between word and deed, between mind and force. One thinks and talks and then later one acts. One experiences thinking and doing as two poles between which one should alternate.

In a trine, two closely related qualities form a friendship and support each other at all times: words are always followed by deeds and one does nothing without also talking – the mind directs the action, the words are powerful, the deeds are skillful.

In a sextile, two planets in zodiacal signs with different but similar qualities occasionally support each other: thoughts have the possibility of becoming actions, and intentions of action have the possibility of making themselves understood to others by words.

In a square, one always reassesses which of the two qualities you want to use in every situation – and the other quality stays out of it completely: mind or force, thought or deed, words or actions.

With a quincunx, thought and action always re-establish order and tension. This leads to the question of how to translate one's own insights into concrete deeds and how to make one's own impulses for action understandable.

In a semi-sextile, either logic or drive pushes for a further development to the respective other quality. As a result, either talk becomes action (Mercury => Mars) or action ends and one begins to think and talk (Mars => Mercury).

Mercury – Jupiter

With a conjunction one experiences no difference between thinking and system: one always thinks in large contexts and with system – and one thinks much and far.

With an opposition, one switches rhythmically back and forth between word and goals, between mind and organization. The individual is viewed independently of the whole, that is, in its independence. However, the systems are also seen – but mainly as that which wants to hinder free thinking.

In a trine, two closely related qualities enter into a friendship and support each other at all times: one thinks in contexts, one sees the individual against the background of the system, one pays attention to the individual elements of what one organizes and manages.

In a sextile, two planets in zodiacal signs with different but similar characteristics occasionally support each other: thoughts have the opportunity to orient and fit into goals, ideals and systems, and goals have the opportunity to make themselves understood by others by words.

With a square, one always reassesses which of the two qualities one wants to use in a given situation – and the other quality stays out of it completely: mind or reason, words or ideals, talking or organizing.

In a quincunx, intellect and reason always re-establish order and tension. This leads to the fact that one strives to be able to make one's own goals understandable to other people by words, and that one wants to support one's own organizing by words – in other words, to ultimately direct one's understanding and life organization towards the same goal, while also taking into account the larger contexts.

In a semi-sextile, either the mind or the ideals urge a progression toward the other quality. This makes either the mind idealistic (Mercury => Jupiter) or the goals factual-rational (Jupiter => Mercury).

Mercury – Saturn

In a conjunction, one experiences no difference between word and foundation: every thought and word is tested for its reality content, and one adopts only those things that are certain; one orients oneself to authorities; one learns from those who already know; one appreciates order, and systematicness in thinking; one orders one's surroundings by factual words that conform to rules.

In opposition, one alternates rhythmically back and forth between word and form, between mind and foundation. What is already known is an obstacle in thinking – it is rather the starting point for discovering something new. But one always returns to the solid shore in between.

In a trine, two closely related qualities enter into a friendship and support each other at all times: One always searches for the principles in thinking or uses the already known principles in thinking. One orients oneself to authorities.

In a sextile, two planets in zodiac signs with different but similar qualities occasionally support each other: the mind has the opportunity to use already existing foundations and information, and the external forms considered important can be well explained and made plausible by words.

With a square, one always reassesses which of the two qualities you want to use in every situation – and the other quality stays out of it completely: insights or principles, thinking or rules, conversations or foundations.

With a quincunx, understanding and life experience always re-establish the order and the tension. This leads one to always wonder if what one is thinking is grounded in reality – or if others just don't understand what one is trying to say. One tends to be a free spirit, but at the same time also to orient oneself to the common world view …

In a semi-sextile, one of the two qualities urges a progression to the other quality. Thus either arguing gives way to accepting the facts (Mercury => Saturn) or the facts are thought through anew (Saturn => Mercury).

Mercury – Uranus

When there is a conjunction, one experiences no difference between thinking and intuition. This gives thinking something lively and jumpy, which not always everyone can follow – sometimes one doesn't even know oneself why one actually knows something.

In an opposition, one switches rhythmically back and forth between logic and spontaneity, between reason and intuition. Sometimes one jumps far into the unknown and discovers new things and at other times one analyzes the known step by step. One feels the intuition as a necessary enrichment of thinking – therefore one makes again and again excursions into the unknown and tries to find new things, in order to settle down afterwards however again in the known and to consider the found at one's leisure.

In a trine, two closely related qualities enter into a friendship and support each other at all times: the logical steps increase again and again to the ingenious leap and the ingenious leap is then broken down into logical steps. You never know where the conversation will lead and what will come next.

In a sextile, two planets in zodiac signs with different but similar qualities occasionally support each other: the mind has the opportunity to get intuition to help it, and intuition has the opportunity to make what it has found understandable to others by words.

With a square, in every situation one always checks anew which of the two qualities one wants to use – and the other quality stays completely out of it: logic or intuition, steps or leaps, clarity or spontaneity.

In a quincunx, reason and intuition always re-establish order and tension. This occasionally leads to situations in which the others can no longer follow you and you first have to explain how you have now so suddenly come to a different view. Sometimes you don't know yourself why you are suddenly convinced of something completely different then before. Possibly one says also for the sake of simplicity that the said is not logical, but that one knows that it is correct – by this one protects oneself against the opinions of the others.

In a semi-sextile, either the mind or the intuition urges a progression to the other quality. Thus either the mind becomes spontaneous-jumpy-intuitive (Mercury => Uranus) or the intuition slows down to step-by-step logic (Uranus => Mercury).

Mercury – Neptune

With a conjunction, one experiences no difference between thinking and foreboding. It is enough for one to have impressions, to orient oneself to vague ideas, to experience a few fragments – and can thus find one's way dreamlike.

In an opposition, one switches rhythmically back and forth between logic and fantasy, between understanding and borderline dissolution. One is addressed by something and experiences oneself as connected with it – thereupon one looks at these things closely and analyzes them in a distanced way, in order to enter into a symbiosis with them again afterwards.

In a trine, two closely related qualities enter into a friendship and support each other at all times: The mind gropes its way to the goal through hunches in a sleepwalking manner. Art, ecology, social issues and religion are logically examined and formulated.

With a sextile, two planets in zodiacal signs with different but similar qualities occasionally support each other: the mind has the possibility of getting the sense of the situation to help it, and anything that dissolves borderlines has the possibility of making itself understood to others by words.

With a square, one always checks anew in every situation which of the two qualities one wants to use – and the other quality stays completely out of it: concept or imagination, geometry or art, knowledge or anticipation.

In a quincunx, reason and imagination always re-establish the order and the tension. This leads to a mixture of logic and foreboding, which is mainly used in art, in the social, in religion and in ecology. From time to time, however, it is necessary to put also the hunches into clear words, which is not always easy.

In a semi-sextile, either the mind or the imagination urges a progression to the other quality. Thus either the mind becomes hunches (Mercury => Neptune) or the hunches become rational arguments (Neptune => Mercury).

Mercury – Pluto

When there is a conjunction, one does not experience a difference between words and the existential. Language serves to identify the essential and to assert the essential: spies, provocateurs, politicos, agitators, corporate executives …

In an opposition, one switches rhythmically back and forth between logic and conviction, between reason and the existential. One may well think calmly about a subject, but afterwards one also commits oneself to the subject again with full force, whereby arguments are not particularly important to oneself – one simply follows one's own conviction.

In a trine, two closely related qualities enter into a friendship and support each other at all times: the mind grasps the essential, which is why words have a very great power of persuasion.

In a sextile, two planets in zodiac signs with different but similar qualities occasionally support each other: the mind has the ability to focus on the essential, and the essential has the ability to express itself by words.

In a square, one always reassesses which of the two qualities one wants to use in a given situation – and the other quality stays out of it completely: science or conviction, logic or necessity, technique or magic.

In a quincunx, reason and conviction are always re-establishing order and tension. This occasionally leads to fierce exchanges of words, where it is not easy to still recognize why one actually wants what. Then a pause and attentive explaining or listening is conducive …

In a semi-sextile either the mind or the basic beliefs push for a further development to the respective other quality. Thus either the mind gives way to inner necessity (Mercury => Pluto) or the basic convictions concretize themselves in rational considerations (Pluto => Mercury).

IX 3. c) Venus

Venus – Sun

In a conjunction, one experiences no difference between feeling and identity – one is what one feels, and one feels what one is … one is an emotional person and one knows oneself by one's feelings. Hiding feelings? How is that supposed to work?

The opposition, trine, sextile, square and quincunx are not possible between the Sun and Mercury, because the maximum distance between them as seen from Earth (as they appear in the chart) is 45° – so only the conjunction (0°) and the semi-sextile (30°) are possible.

In a semi-sextile, either the feeling or the self-expression pushes for a progression to the other quality. Thus either the feeling becomes egocentric (Venus => Sun) or the self-expression becomes emotional (Sun => Venus).

Venus – Mars

In a conjunction one experiences no difference between feelings and actions, between eroticism and sex, between affection and ecstasy … one is very emotional in any action – both emotional in expression and sensitive … and one therefore needs beautiful life circumstances for one's actions …

In an opposition one alternates rhythmically back and forth between feeling and force, between evaluation and action. One finds someone likeable and also shows it to him … and at some point one changes into action and wants to experience sex with him, go on a hike or work with him.

In a trine, two closely related qualities form a friendship and support each other at all times: the sense of beauty joins with the sense of action, making the actions charming and the beauty powerful – love and sex combine for a hearty, fiery encounter.

In a sextile, two planets in zodiac signs with different but similar qualities occasionally support each other: feelings have the opportunity to become action, and actions have the opportunity to become soulful – thus love and sex, among other things, can be combined.

With a square you always check anew in every situation which of the two qualities you want to use – and the other quality stays completely out of it: love or sex, feeling or action, sympathy or aggression.

In a quincunx, feelings and deeds always have to re-establish order and tension. This can lead, among other things, to the fact that occasionally sex forgets love and must first find it again – or also that love loses sight of sex. As with all quincunxes, the most helpful thing then is to pause, pay attention and be sensitive.

In a semi-sextile, either the feeling or the drive pushes for a further development to the respective other quality. Thus either love becomes sex or more generally formulated the feeling becomes action (Venus => Mars) or the actions end and dissolve into feelings (Mars => Venus).

Venus – Jupiter

In a <u>conjunction</u>, one experiences no difference between feelings and organization: one creates out of all feelings about all people and all things a large, comprehensive feeling attitude in which there is room for everyone and everything. One can organize only when one is emotionally involved in the subject at hand.

In an <u>opposition</u>, one shifts rhythmically back and forth between feeling and goal, between evaluation and organization. One looks at what one wants to achieve, and organizes that – and then switches to feeling and pours over what has been achieved, or feels about what else one would like to have in one's life.

In a <u>trine</u>, two closely related qualities enter into a friendship and support each other at all times: one organizes one's feelings, one builds one's sympathies into a system, one manages one's shifting love relationships. The organization serves the development of the feelings and the feelings strive to be connected into a great overall attitude.

In a <u>sextile</u>, two planets in zodiac signs with different but similar characteristics occasionally support each other: feelings have the opportunity to become real experiences by the talent for organization, and one's goals will, in most cases, take into account one's feelings and preferences.

With a <u>square</u>, one always reassesses which of the two qualities one wants to use in a given situation – and the other quality stays out of it completely: feeling or ideal, love or life organization, liking or goals.

In a <u>quincunx</u>, feeling and life planning always re-establish order and tension. This can mean that love and general life goals are sometimes difficult to reconcile. However, if you take care not to become hard and tense or weak and resigned, but remain strong and elastic, these contradictions can be resolved after a while in most cases.

In a <u>semi-sextile</u>, either the feeling or the ideals push for a further development to the respective other quality. Thus either the feeling becomes idealistic (Venus => Jupiter) or the ideals become emotional (Jupiter => Venus).

Venus – Saturn

In a <u>conjunction</u>, one experiences no difference between feelings and permanence. When you feel something, it is forever … chronic emotions … In the realm of feelings, one always wants to know exactly where one stands and what the other person is feeling.

In an <u>opposition</u>, one alternates rhythmically back and forth between feeling and foundation, between evaluation and preservation. One is alternately charming-seductive and hard-principled – depending on which side of the "swing" one is at the moment.

In a trine, two closely related qualities form a friendship and support each other at all times: feelings are permanent and everything permanent is filled with feelings. One is emotionally stable and faithful and seeks firm, secure and clearly defined emotional relationships.

In a sextile, two planets in zodiac signs with different but similar qualities occasionally support each other: feelings have the possibility of finding or creating a suitable outer form for themselves, and the forms have the possibility of being a solid foundation for the feelings.

With a square, one always reassesses which of the two qualities one wants to use in a given situation – and the other quality stays out of it completely: following the feelings or consistency, sympathy or principle, love or security.

In a quincunx, feelings and form always re-establish order and tension. This occasionally leads to doubts about one's own feeling-reliability: "Do you still love me?" Again, developing the previous form according to the new circumstances is what helps.

In a semi-sextile, either feeling or life experience urges further development to the other quality. Thus either the feeling becomes objective (Venus => Saturn) or the life experience becomes feelings (Saturn => Venus).

Venus – Uranus

In a conjunction, one experiences no difference between feelings and intuitions, since intuitions come from feelings and feelings develop by leaps and bounds – spontaneous emotions.

With an opposition, one alternates rhythmically back and forth between feeling and intuition, between evaluation and spontaneity. Both are experienced as different, but as part of a constant vibration – sometimes one feels and sometimes one follows a spontaneous impulse.

In a trine, two closely related qualities enter into a friendship and support each other at all times: feelings blossom in spontaneity and everything sudden and new is primarily a feeling.

In a sextile, two planets in zodiac signs with different but similar qualities occasionally support each other: feelings can sometimes become very spontaneous, and intuition has the ability of being grasped by feelings and expressed by feelings.

With a square, one always checks anew in every situation which of the two qualities one wants to use – and the other quality stays completely out of it: feeling or intuition, love or spontaneity, sympathy or novelty.

In a quincunx, feelings and spontaneity always re-establish order and tension. This leads to entertaining relationships (viewed from the outside) and occasional doubts about one's love (viewed from the inside). However, sincere and attentive introspection can bring clarity to these often quite turbulent emotional situations.

In a semi-sextile either the feeling or the spontaneity pushes for a further development to the other quality. Thus either the feeling becomes spontaneous-jumpy-curious (Venus => Uranus) or the spontaneity becomes feelings (Uranus => Venus).

Venus – Neptune

In a conjunction one experiences no difference between feelings and the dissolution of boundaries, since all feelings expand into the vastness and have no limiting measure – thus in any dissolution of boundaries, as in magic, mysticism, social engagement, art, ecology, one is always carried by one's own feelings.

In an opposition one switches rhythmically back and forth between feeling and imagination, between evaluation and sympathy. Love and the artistic representation of love alternate, as do the pursuit of beauty and the pursuit of widening consciousness, and also individual affection and general social engagement.

In a trine, two closely related qualities enter into a friendship and support each other at all times: feelings are the gateway to the vastness of the world; feelings are the gateway to art, to communities, to religion, and to ecology. On the other hand, experiencing connectedness with the whole always leads to feelings: Contact with the world is feeling – bhakti yoga …

In a sextile, two planets in zodiac signs with different but similar qualities occasionally support each other: individual love has the possibility to become a general love of man, and this connectedness with the whole can also concretize into a feeling for an individual.

With a square, one always checks anew in every situation which of the two qualities one wants to use – and the other quality stays completely out of it: feeling or hunch, love or art, preferences or ecology.

In a quincunx, feeling and imagination always re-establish order and tension. This sometimes leads to daydreaming of feelings or relationships that aren't there in real life – both longings and fears. Here the distinction between dreams and reality is needed – and the search for a meaningful next step to get closer to the realization of dreams.

In a semi-sextile, either the feeling or the boundary dissolving urges a progression to the other quality. Thereby either the individual feeling is widened to general feelings, i.e. the love for a concrete person becomes general human love (Venus => Neptune) or one narrows these general feelings to a concrete feeling and thereby concretizes them (Neptune => Venus).

Venus – Pluto

In a <u>conjunction</u> one experiences no difference between feelings and the essential, because feelings are the essential and everything essential expresses itself by feelings – how could it be otherwise? Love is existential – and so is dislike …

In an <u>opposition</u> one switches rhythmically back and forth between feeling and conviction, between evaluation and existential. Sometimes one follows one's love and sometimes one follows one's basic convictions – both can be very different, but are still experienced as belonging together.

In a <u>trine</u>, two closely related qualities enter into a friendship and support each other at all times: feelings increase to existential and are the access to the essential, which always shows itself first by feelings. Feelings are what make the world go round.

In a <u>sextile</u>, two planets in zodiac signs with different but similar qualities occasionally support each other: feelings have the possibility to become intense, and the essential has the possibility to be experienced as feelings.

With a <u>square</u>, one always reassesses which of the two qualities one wants to use in a given situation – and the other quality stays out of it completely: feeling or conviction, sympathy or essentials, beauty or essence.

In a <u>quincunx</u>, feelings and convictions always re-establish order and tension. This leads to intense feelings, which sometimes cannot be too firmly founded in reality – then pausing and introspection, as well as talking as calmly as possible with the people who may be involved, is beneficial.

In a <u>semi-sextile</u>, either the feeling or the basic beliefs urge a progression to the respective other quality. Thus either the feeling becomes existential (Venus => Pluto) or the basic convictions become feelings (Pluto => Venus).

IX 3. d) Sun

Sun – Mars

In a <u>conjunction</u> one experiences no difference between identity and action – one always does what one wants, and one experiences oneself as what one does. One can only act self-determined – otherwise one simply has no power …

In an <u>opposition</u>, one alternates rhythmically back and forth between center and force, between self-expression and action: sometimes one reflects on what one wants, and sometimes one does what one wants. The alternation here is not in the realm of self-fidelity, but in the fact that one alternately feels into oneself and acts.

In a trine, two closely related qualities enter into a friendship and support each other at all times: if one wants to do something, one does it. And one doesn't do anything one doesn't want to do. That's all there is to it!

In a sextile, two planets in zodiac signs with different but similar qualities occasionally support each other: the ego has the opportunity to express itself by deeds, and the deeds have the opportunity to become self-expression.

In a square, one always reassesses which of the two qualities one wants to use in every situation – and the other quality stays out of it completely: ego or deed, self-expression or drives, self-realization or struggle.

In a quincunx, ego and deed always re-establish the order and the tension. This leads to the question of how to do what you actually experience yourself as: "How can I always do what I want?" One sometimes has the feeling of not being able to be true to oneself in one's deeds – then it is necessary to reflect and look for a meaningful next step, for a first step on the path that corresponds to oneself … and on which one must stop and look again and again in order to readjust one's own course.

In a semi-sextile, either self-expression or drive urges a progression to the other quality. Thus either the self-expression becomes deeds or a little more specially formulated, the perception of the being of the other person becomes sex with him (Sun => Mars) or the deeds become egocentric (Mars => Sun).

Sun – Jupiter

With a conjunction, one experiences no difference between identity and organization: one is the one who organizes, and what one organizes is always self-expression – and one is always the one who organizes, for how should one be able to let another determine one's goals and the way to get there without losing oneself in the process?

In an opposition, one alternates rhythmically back and forth between center and goal, between self-expression and organization. Here the poles are the individual and the superordinate – one takes care of both, but not at the same time, and one does not connect both to a unity, but always lets them be two separate areas of life.

In a trine, two closely related qualities enter into a friendship and support each other at all times: one experiences oneself as part of a system, as part of a group – one organizes the life one wants to live and is the manager of one's own course of life, whose reins one holds firmly in one's hand.

In a sextile, two planets in zodiacal signs with different but similar qualities occasionally support each other: the ego has the opportunity to shape itself as a total life design, and the organizational talent necessary for this has the opportunity to orient itself to what one wants.

With a square, one always re-examines which of the two qualities one wants to use in a given situation – and the other quality stays completely out of it: self-expression or life organization, ego or goals, egocentricity or ideals.

In a quincunx, self-expression and life-organization constantly re-establish order and tension. This occasionally leads to contradictions between what one wants and what one thinks is right – whereupon a reorientation is called for, in which this contradiction may be resolved …

In a semi-sextile, either self-expression or ideals urge a progression to the other quality. As a result, either the self-expression gives way to the ideals (Sun => Jupiter) or the ideals become egocentric (Mars => Sun).

Sun – Saturn

In a conjunction one experiences no difference between identity and form, since one experiences oneself as the permanent thing in the world – one is that which arises out of the regularities of the world. Consequently, one sees oneself as permanent and as hardly changeable.

In an opposition, one alternates rhythmically back and forth between center and supporting form, between self-expression and preservation, between heart and bone. One sees on the one hand the life urge in one's own inner being and on the other hand the outer necessities and takes care of both alternately, so that both can flourish.

In a trine, two closely related qualities enter into a friendship and support each other at all times: will and destiny combine, will becomes form and form becomes will – one creates a well-defined, solid, enduring shape of one's self-expression.

In a sextile, two planets in zodiacal signs with different but similar qualities occasionally support each other: the ego has the possibility of becoming a fixed, defined form, and for external forms there is the possibility that the ego identifies with them.

With a square, one always checks anew in every situation which of the two qualities one wants to use – and the other quality stays completely out of it: self-expression or laws, will or rules, the "I" or constancy.

In a quincunx, will and law always re-establish order and tension. This leads to a struggle of the will with the external circumstances, in which one finds again and again well livable compromises and cooperations, which however all do not last forever, but only work temporarily – and then must be formulated again.

In a semi-sextile, either self-expression or realism pushes for further development toward the other quality. As a result, either self-expression gives way to accepting the world as it is (Sun => Saturn) or one no longer cares about life experiences and just does what one wants (Saturn => Sun).

Sun – Uranus

With a conjunction, one experiences no difference between center and eccentric. One is always something else, something new – each identity is only one of many possibilities ...

With an opposition, one shifts rhythmically back and forth between center and eccentric, between self-expression and curiosity. The centric and the eccentric cross-fertilize each other: one is alternately focused entirely on self-expression and on discovering and conquering new territory.

In a trine, two closely related qualities enter into a friendship and support each other at all times: one is many things – and above all, one is all that one could become. The center is eccentric ... and constantly new and different. Why limit yourself to any self-definition?

In a sextile, two planets in zodiac signs with different but similar qualities occasionally support each other: the ego has the opportunity to spontaneously reinvent and redefine itself, and spontaneous intuition has the opportunity to become self-expression.

With a square, one always reassesses which of the two qualities one wants to use in a given situation – and the other quality stays out of it completely: center or eccentricity, self-expression or spontaneity, identity or novelty.

In a quincunx, the center and the eccentricity always re-establish the order and the tension. This often leads to the question, "Who am I? And if so, how many?" One usually has more than one self-image or personality, and there is therefore the task of coordinating this multiplicity of inner possibilities into a sonorous concert as a conductor.

In a semi-sextile, either self-expression or intuition urges a progression to the other quality. As a result, either self-expression gives way to spontaneity (Sun => Uranus) or spontaneity gives way to egocentricity (Uranus => Sun).

Sun – Neptune

With a conjunction, one experiences no difference between identity and expansiveness: one experiences oneself in art, in social engagement, in meditation in ecology ... The ego is a drop in a boundless sea and is real but has no delineated identity ... one distinguishes only slightly between oneself and the rest of the world ...

In an opposition, one alternates rhythmically back and forth between center and boundary dissolution, between self-expression and sympathy. Here egoism and altruism replace each other again and again – one is alternating focused on one's own well-being and the well-being of the community. As always with an opposition, the essential point is the harmonious rhythm that ensures that both areas receive a some-what equal attention.

In a trine, two closely related qualities enter into a friendship and support each other at all times: the ego is experienced as part of the whole, as part of the continuum, as a drop in the ocean, as a wave in the flow of life – one is connected to everything and has no existence or individuality in oneself, but exists only as a part of the whole, which is what is actually real. One is community, spirituality, art, ecology …

In a sextile, two planets in zodiacal signs with different but similar qualities occa-sionally support each other: egoism has the possibility to widen into altruism, and the sense of connection with the whole has the possibility to become self-expression.

With a square, one is always testing anew in a given situation which of the two qualities one wante to use – and the other quality stays completely out of it: egocen-trism or boundary dissolution, self-expression or art, self-expression or socially com-patible behavior.

In a quincunx, centering and boundary dissolution keep re-establishing order and tension. This leads ultimately to the experience of having a quality but no boundary – an experience that occurs in more advanced meditations. It is the search for what one is within the whole.

In a semi-sextile, either self-expression or boundary dissolution urges a progression to the other quality. As a result, either self-expression gives way to expansion (Sun => Neptune) or the perception of all-connectedness narrows to an egocentricity (Neptune => Sun).

Sun – Pluto

In a conjunction one experiences no difference between the ego and the essential, because one's own ego is the essential, it is what one wants to live and express. Indi-viduality is the essence of life … and one has no problems at all to enforce what one wants …

In an opposition, one shifts rhythmically back and forth between center and origin, between self-expression and self-preservation. At some times you just live what you like, and at other times you do what is necessary for survival. One experiences "living one's life" and "doing what is essential" as two poles of a whole.

In a trine, two closely related qualities enter into a friendship and support each other at all times: the self is the essence, one's will is the center of life, one is the essence of the world – it is all about self-expression.

In a sextile, two planets in zodiac signs with different but similar qualities occasio-nally support each other: the "I" has the possibility to be experienced as the essence, and the essence has the possibility to be experienced as one's source.

92

With a square, one is always testing anew in every situation which of the two qualities one wants to use – and the other quality stays completely out of it: self-expression or striving for the essential, ego or God, egoism or ecology.

In a quincunx, self-expression and basic convictions always re-establish the order and the tension. This leads to the fact that one asks oneself again and again how one can unite one's own desires and preferences with what one considers to be essential. Contemplative hours, conversations with friends or meditations are always helpful.

In a semi-sextile, either self-expression or basic beliefs urge a progression to the other quality. Thus either self-expression gives way to basic beliefs (Sun => Pluto) or basic beliefs are put on the back burner in favor of egoism (Pluto => Sun).

IX 3. e) Mars

Mars – Jupiter

With a conjunction one experiences no difference between action and organization, between power and energy, between action and goal – both are united: One knows what one wants, recognizes the way to it and goes it. Quite simply …

In an opposition, one alternates rhythmically back and forth between action and goal, between force and energy. The times of searching for the right goal are the basis of the times of realizing those goals by action – and the times of action, in turn, inspire the times of grasping the best possible goals.

In a trine, two closely related qualities enter into a friendship and support each other at all times: the individual deed is always seen against the background of the higher goals – it therefore becomes the realization of the ideals. The goals and ideals, for their part, are entirely geared towards their energetic realization. It is organized and managed with power and if necessary also with aggression.

In a sextile, two planets in zodiac signs with different but similar qualities occasionally support each other: the deeds have the possibility of being supported by the organizational talent, and one's ideals and goals have the possibility of being realized by the energy.

With a square, one always reassesses which of the two qualities one wante to use in a given situation – and the other quality stays completely out of it: deed or ideal, competition or cooperation, sex or collegiality.

With a quincunx, one has always to restore order and tension between drive and organizational talent. This leads to the fact that one often wants to do something different than what would be conducive to the achievement of one's goals. Then it is necessary to see how one can bring this together, for what one wants to spend how much time and in which areas of life one wants to live these two impulses.

In a semi-sextile either the drive or the higher goals push for a further development to the respective other quality. Thus either the drive gives way to the organization of life (Mars => Jupiter) or pragmatic deeds take the place of ideals (Jupiter => Mars).

Mars – Saturn

In a conjunction one experiences no difference between force and form. One immediately recognizes which form is optimal to use one's power, one creates forms by one's actions; and one needs clarity to effectively direct one's power.

In an opposition, one alternates rhythmically back and forth between action and form, between force and foundation. When one acts, one steps out of tradition and rules and completely follows one's own impulse to act – but this is always followed by a placement in the fabric of life, in which everything receives its place … until one steps out of the formed again and simply acts.

In a trine, two closely related qualities form a friendship and support each other at all times: actions are always persistent and emphatic and formed in the most effective way. Actions always have a larger framework to guide them. Principles are carried out with great vigor. A marathon runner …

In a sextile, two planets in zodiac signs with different but similar qualities occasionally support each other: the deeds have the opportunity to be given a supportive foundation by the outer forms, and the outer forms have the opportunity to be protected and strengthened by the deeds.

With a square, one always reassesses which of the two qualities one wants to use in a given situation – and the other quality stays out of it completely: sex or marriage, drive or law, free action or legality.

In a quincunx, force and form always restore order and tension. This leads to the fact that one often transgresses rules or comes into conflict with the law. It makes sense to take a closer look at the outer situations and the inner impulses as early as possible and to look for possibilities to keep the conflicts as low as possible and with few consequences.

In a semi-sextile, either drive or life experience urges a progression to the other quality. Thus either drive gives way to life experience and acceptance of circumstances (Mars => Saturn) or drive takes the place of acceptance of life circumstances (Saturn => Mars).

Mars – Uranus

With a <u>conjunction</u> one experiences no difference between force and spontaneity, because on the one hand force is always used spontaneously and intuitively, and on the other hand intuition always appears when acting. One is always open to new ways of acting, to new ways of doing things, to experimentation in sex....

In an <u>opposition,</u> one alternates rhythmically back and forth between action and spontaneity, between force and changing course. The purposeful action and the striving for something new alternate, whereby in a rhythmic way on the one hand the course of action and on the other hand the direction of intuition is changed.

In a <u>trine,</u> two closely related qualities enter into a friendship and support each other at all times: drive is most effective when it is spontaneous – intuitions always result immediately in action. One acts unpredictably, one acts in always new ways, one's actions cannot be predicted by others (and neither by oneself).

In a <u>sextile</u>, two planets in zodiac signs with different but similar qualities occasionally support each other: action has the possibility of finding new ways by intuition, and intuition has the possibility of not remaining just an abstract idea by action.

With a <u>square</u>, one always checks anew in every situation which of the two qualities one wants to use – and the other quality stays completely out of it: deed or intuition, anger or spontaneity, action or rediscovery.

In a <u>quincunx</u>, action and spontaneity always restore order and tension. This leads to frequent changes of course, by which one is possibly also surprised oneself. Here it is beneficial to bring a little alertness into the whole, without thereby impairing the drive or spontaneity – this is a task for the director, who in the end is always the one who can make sure that one lives the aspects in one's horoscope in the most constructive and fruitful way possible.

In a <u>semi-sextile</u>, either drive or intuition urges a progression to the other quality. Thus, either drive gives way to spontaneous impulses (Mars => Uranus) or action takes the place of spontaneity (Uranus => Mars).

Mars – Neptune

With a <u>conjunction</u> one experiences no difference between deed and boundary dissolution, which means that one always acts with regard to the whole and that one always experiences any artistic, social, religious or ecological commitment as deeds, i.e. as an expression of power – one does something that is related to the whole.

In an <u>opposition</u>, one alternates rhythmically back and forth between deed and imagination, between force and sympathy. Aggression and altruism replace each other: energy and compassion, sexuality and art, desire and ecology, anger and religion …

and both always cross-fertilize each other.

In a trine, two closely related qualities enter into a friendship and support each other at all times: action follows the sense of the most sensible path, which one senses rather than really knows. Any mysticism, art, social commitment and religion wants to become deed.

In a sextile, two planets in zodiacs with different but similar qualities occasionally support each other: action has the possibility of expanding into altruistic action, and sexuality can lead to enlightenment through the by of kundalini and by tantra yoga; and on the other hand, social engagement, spirituality, ecology, and art have the possibility of making a great impact and changing the world by action.

With a square, one always reassesses which of the two qualities one wants to use in a given situation – and the other quality stays out of it completely: sexual desire or symbiotic love, drives or social consideration, horniness or art.

In a quincunx, drive and imagination always restore order and tension. This sometimes leads to the fact that one exerts oneself too much for one's social, religious, artistic or ecological commitments – this should be avoided and one should take one's power level as important as the just mentioned commitments. And one should also give enough space in one's life to the simple enjoyment of power in laughter, dance and sex.

In a semi-sextile, either the drive or the wishful dreams push for a further development to the respective other quality. Thus either the drive gives way to daydreaming, which can be quite productive, (Mars => Neptune) or the fantasy condenses into concrete deeds (Neptune => Mars).

Mars – Pluto

With a conjunction one experiences no difference between deed and existential. As Goethe said, "In the beginning was the deed." Or Heraclitus, "War is the father of all things." One has the tendency to place action, sexuality, ecstasy, struggle at the center of one's life.

In an opposition, one alternates rhythmically back and forth between action and conviction, between force and existential necessity. Here, acting out of the urge to act is followed by a focus on the essential and existential, which is then followed by acting out of simple need again after a while.

In a trine, two closely related qualities enter into a friendship and support each other at all times: every action is directed towards the essential and all existential topics become action. As a result, action is always intense, fierce, single-minded, unwavering, and full of power.

In a sextile, two planets in zodiacal signs with different but similar qualities occasionally support each other: deeds have the possibility to become single-minded, and the essential has the possibility to appear as concrete action in the world.

With a square, one always checks anew in every situation which of the two qualities one wants to use – and the other quality stays completely out of it: deed or conviction, action or reflection on the essential, revenge or self-transformation.

In a quincunx, one always has to re-establish order and tension between force and conviction. This may lead sometimes to not knowing what you actually want to do – or to being completely fixated on some actions. In both cases it is necessary to calmly sense and consider one's own impulses for action and basic convictions in order to get back on a clear course.

In a semi-sextile, either the drive or the basic convictions urge further development to the other quality. Thus either the energy gives way to the orientation towards the essential (Mars => Pluto) or one leaves aside the grasping of the essential and steps into action (Pluto => Mars).

IX 3. f) Jupiter

Jupiter – Saturn

In a conjunction one experiences no difference between organization and form – after all, everything that one has organized is also given a solid form ... and how should one be able to make something solid if one hasn't chosen and organized it first? Obviously, the values and the goals are very constant here.

In an opposition, one alternates rhythmically between goal and form, between organizing and maintaining. Organizing and managing lead to fixed forms, which are then preserved and protected; after a while, however, the urge for new goals and projects arises and one breaks away from the existing forms and builds something new ... which one then transfers again into a fixed form.

In a trine, two closely related qualities form a friendship and support each other at all times: organizing the achievement of one's goals is always based on reality and on using the rules and authorities to achieve them. The goals are consistent and one becomes a part of the system that maintains the form.

In a sextile, two planets in zodiac signs with different but similar characteristics occasionally support each other: the life organization has the ability to create solid forms, and the form has the ability to promote the achievement of one's goals.

With a square, one always checks anew in every situation which of the two qualities one wants to use – and the other quality stays completely out of it: organization or rule-keeping, ideal or tradition, self-organization or incorporation.

In a quincunx, organizational ability and necessities always re-establish order and tension. That leads to the fact that one looks again and again for possibilities, how one can convert what one wants, in view of the external situation nevertheless. Creativity is required here above all.

In a semi-sextile either the organization of life or the experience of life urge a further development to the respective other quality. Thus either the ideal gives way to the acceptance of the life circumstances (Jupiter => Saturn) or the ideals push past the acceptance of the apparently inevitable into the foreground (Saturn => Jupiter).

Jupiter – Uranus

With a conjunction one experiences no difference between organization and intuition: The organization follows the intuition and one wants to realize everything, which one intuitively grasps as good, also by one's own organizing. The course of one's life is thus a bit erratic, but rich in interesting turns.

In the case of an opposition, one alternates rhythmically back and forth between goal and idea, between organization and spontaneity. The organizing goes on steadily for a while and is then suddenly whirled through by new ideas; but after a while the new begins to concretize itself in clear forms and becomes organizable and directable … until a new idea puts everything into turbulence again.

In a trine, two closely related qualities form a friendship and support each other at all times: goals are always new – every time one discovers a new possibility, ideal, or goal, and organizes change.

In a sextile, two planets in zodiacal signs with different but similar qualities occasionally support each other: managing the realization of one's ideals has the possibility of following spontaneous intuitions, thus enriching oneself with new aspects and finding shortcuts, and intuition has the possibility of fitting into the already existing system, enriching and developing it.

In a square, one always checks anew in every situation which of the two qualities one wants to use – and the other quality stays completely out of it: Ideal or inspiration, construction or sudden change, design or invention.

In a quincunx, goals and spontaneity constantly restore order and tension. This can lead to frequent changes of course, none of which are of great permanence. All of these changes come about because of new circumstances that are integrated into the previous course, thus preserving the effectiveness of one's course. For this, however, a great alertness is necessary, so that one's own goals are changed in time, but also not hastily.

In a semi-sextile, either life organization or intuition urge further development towards the other quality. Thus either the ideal gives way to the new (Jupiter => Uranus) or the new fades away and one goes over to organizing one's own life (Uranus => Jupiter).

Jupiter – Neptune

With a <u>conjunction</u> one experiences no difference between organization and dissolution of boundaries. One always seeks universal values and goals and one always organizes for all; one wants the all-encompassing community to emerge.

In an <u>opposition</u>, one alternates rhythmically back and forth between goal and participation, between organization and boundary dissolution. Financing and art alternate, and so do management and charitable commitment, community organization and spiritual striving, self-sufficiency and ecology, and so on.

In a <u>trine</u>, two closely related qualities enter into a friendship and support each other at all times: when one organizes something, it always expands to improve the general situation, not just one's own. One has the gift to realize all social, religious, ecological and artistic goals, with the help of one's management ability.

In a <u>sextile</u>, two planets in zodiacal signs with different but similar qualities occasionally support each other: organizing has the possibility of pursuing generally desirable goals, and community desire, art, religion, and ecology have the possibility of being realized by the design of systems and organizations.

With a <u>square</u>, one always reassesses which of the two qualities one wants to use in a given situation – and the other quality stays completely out of it: community or spirituality, system organization or art, corporate success or ecologically correct behavior.

In a <u>quincunx</u>, ideals and dream images always re-establish the order and the tension. This leads to the danger of striving for the impossible – you have to look at all projects, how you want to approach it and what is the most effective way … whereby you can also use magic once in a while.

In a <u>semi-sextile</u> either the life organization or the border resolution pushes for a further development to the respective other quality. Thereby either the ideal gives way to the immersion in the experience of being one with the whole (Jupiter => Neptune) or one returns from the vastness of fantasy to the organizing of everyday life (Neptune => Jupiter).

Jupiter – Pluto

With a <u>conjunction</u> one experiences no difference between organization and existential. This means that one's values and goals are universal and should be enforced in a general way. In doing so, one can be decidedly persuasive and effective … and hopefully not too dominant.

In an <u>opposition</u> one alternates rhythmically back and forth between goal and existential necessity, between organization and vocation. Sometimes you strive for the deepest roots of the world and sometimes you simply regulate your own everyday life …

In a <u>trine</u>, two closely related qualities enter into a friendship and support each other at all times: one's goals always express the existential and are therefore of great persuasiveness and associated with a great ability to assert oneself. Everything essential is immediately formulated in implementation plans, which are then propagated and realized.

In a <u>sextile</u>, two planets in zodiacal signs with different but similar characteristics occasionally support each other: one's own goals have the possibility of becoming general goals, and the essential has the possibility of attaining an external form as an organization.

With a <u>square</u>, one always checks anew in every situation which of the two qualities one wants to use – and the other quality stays completely out of it: ideal or conviction, organization or transformation, goal or necessity of life.

In a <u>quincunx</u>, ideals and basic convictions always re-establish the order and the tension. This leads to the necessity of coordinating what one would like to have oneself (the ideals of Jupiter) with the basic beliefs and necessities (Pluto). If one succeeds in this, one's own management of life's circumstances has a great success – but it is necessary to coordinate both again and again, because with quincunxes there are never final solutions, but always only the next sensible step.

In a <u>semi-sextile</u> either the life organization or the basic beliefs push for a further development to the respective other quality. Thus either the ideal gives way to what one experiences as existential (Jupiter => Pluto) or the basic convictions fade and give way to the pursuit of personal ideals (Pluto => Jupiter).

IX 3. g) Saturn

Saturn – Uranus

In a <u>conjunction</u> one experiences no difference between form and invention, between the old and the new, between the tried and true and experimentation. One uses one's own experience as a springboard into the unknown, and one thoroughly examines the new in order to incorporate it into one's own experience.

In an <u>opposition</u>, one shifts rhythmically back and forth between form and form-bursting, between foundation and realignment. At times one stands firm as a sentinel at the city wall and at other times one bounces curiously through the unknown areas outside the city. In this way, one alternately preserves one's fundament and enriches oneself by discovering and experiencing new possibilities.

In a <u>trine</u>, two closely related qualities enter into a friendship and support each other at all times: the form absorbs every new insight and impulse and thus expands into a more comprehensive form. Therefore, there are no fixed rules, but only the rules that express the state of current knowledge and development.

In a <u>sextile</u>, two planets in zodiacal signs with different but similar characteristics occasionally support each other: the existing has the possibility to be expanded by the new, and the new has the possibility to join with the already existing.

With a <u>square</u>, one always checks anew in every situation which of the two qualities one wants to use – and the other quality stays completely out of it: regulation or intuitive behavior, rules or spontaneity, tradition or progress.

In a <u>quincunx</u>, tradition and invention always provide the order and the tension anew. This leads to the fact that very often it must be examined whether a new idea is really helpful and if so, how it can be integrated best into the existing without losing the advantages of the already existing.

In a <u>semi-sextile</u>, either life experience or intuition pushes for a further development towards the other quality. Thus either the search for security gives way to the desire for the new (Saturn => Uranus) or one loses interest in the new and returns to the old (Uranus => Saturn).

Saturn – Neptune

In a <u>conjunction</u>, one experiences no difference between the boundary and the dissolution of the boundary. The dissolution of the boundary becomes the system, the foundation – one wants to widen the existing through art, religion, social engagement and ecology, because one experiences only the all-encompassing, boundaryless wideness as the real foundation of all things.

In an opposition, one alternates rhythmically back and forth between form and fantasy, between foundation and dissolution of boundaries. Here tradition and free art replace each other and likewise state care and individual help, official regulations and ecological commitment, religious regulations and one's own spiritual experience.

In a trine, two closely related qualities enter into a friendship and support each other at all times: social commitment, religion, ecology and art need a fixed form to be able to flourish, they need rules to be able to grow, and laws to be able to become real. Fantasy becomes history, daydream becomes reality, magic becomes everyday life.

In a sextile, two planets in zodiacal signs with different but similar characteristics occasionally support each other: the fixed forms have the possibility to give a support and a foundation to spiritual, social, ecological and artistic aspirations, and these aspirations can in turn develop the existing forms and make them come alive – mysticism and magic as a stimulus for the evolution of religion.

With a square, one always checks anew in every situation which of the two qualities one wants to use – and the other quality stays completely out of it: religion or mysticism, tradition or art, precept or hunch.

In a quincunx, the fixed and the imaginative always establish the order and the tension anew. This leads to the question, which rules are useful to reach the superior goal. Here neither the complete self-sacrifice of Neptune nor the hard insistence on the tried and true are conducive, but the constant development of the generally established framework conditions.

In a semi-sextile, either life experience or imagination urge further development toward the other quality. Thereby either the search for security gives way to the desire for width (Saturn => Neptune) or one loses the interest in width and returns to the well-tried (Neptune => Saturn).

Saturn – Pluto

With a conjunction one experiences no difference between form and the existential, because it is the existential which brings forth the form. Consequently, one wants to bring everything essential also into a solid form. This can lead to a certain harshness.

In an opposition, one alternates rhythmically back and forth between form and existential necessity, between foundation and essence. Here laws and convictions can enrich each other by knowing and appreciating both.

In a trine, two closely related qualities enter into a friendship and support each other at all times: the laws of nature, the laws of man and the rules by which one lives one's own truth arise from the essence. The solid form is the expression of the innermost essence. Everything fundamental is manifested in the form that creates it, since it is the formative element of that form. Therefore, the essence and its form are one.

In a <u>sextile</u>, two planets in zodiacal signs with different but similar qualities occasionally support each other: the solid forms have the possibility of expressing the essential, and the essential has the possibility of taking a well-defined shape.

With a <u>square</u>, one always checks anew in every situation which of the two qualities one wants to use – and the other quality stays completely out of it: law or conviction, form or content, stabilization or revolution.

In a <u>quincunx</u>, form and substance always re-establish the order and the tension. This leads to the question of which form best promotes what one wants to achieve – without unduly harming other things. This question leads to many shape changes and metamorphoses …

In a <u>semi-sextile</u>, either life experience or basic beliefs urge a progression to the other quality. Thus either the search for security gives way to the desire for existential intensity (Saturn => Pluto) or one loses interest in ecstasy and returns to the familiar (Pluto => Saturn).

IX 3. h)   Uranus

Uranus – Neptune

In a <u>conjunction</u> one experiences no difference between intuition and hunch: the sudden idea leads to a widening of the horizon; spontaneous contact leads to symbiosis; art is always expression in the moment; religion is experiencing the world in the here and now; social engagement can only happen where a need is just occurring; and ecology is helping in the place where a crisis is just occurring.

In <u>opposition</u>, one shifts rhythmically back and forth between spontaneity and sympathy, between intuition and imagination. The new leads to changing one's view of the whole – and the changed view of the whole leads in turn to new discoveries. That which is alternating in this aspect is the leap over the abyss to a very specific place and the sensing into the whole, i.e. the individual unexpected and the resonating with the whole.

In a <u>trine</u>, two closely related qualities enter into a friendship and support each other at all times: intuition broadens foreboding perception; imagination enables new ideas. Therefore, art represents novelty, communities evolve by leaps and bounds, ecology is an adjustment to ever new situations, God's action is unpredictable.

In a <u>sextile</u>, two planets in zodiacal signs with different but similar qualities occasionally support each other: intuition has the possibility to open the door to sense the whole, and boundary dissolving allows the possibility to discover new things.

In a square one always checks anew in every situation which of the two qualities one wants to use – and the other quality stays completely out of it: intuition or hunch, spontaneity or imagination, novelty or sympathy.

In a quincunx, intuition and imagination always restore order and tension. This leads to the question of how to combine the joy of the new and the connection with the whole world into a creative whole.

In a semi-sextile, either intuition or imagination pushes for a further development towards the other quality. As a result, either the desire for something new gives way to the need for a broad connection to the whole (Uranus => Neptune) or one loses interest in the broadening and prefers to simply experience something new (Neptune => Uranus).

Uranus – Pluto

In a conjunction one experiences no difference between intuition and the essential: intuition is the essential and the essential is always grasped only intuitively – and the essential is new in every moment, it is the spontaneous creation of the here and now … every moment is existential, but no two moments are the same …

In an opposition, one alternates rhythmically back and forth between spontaneity and the existential, between intuition and grasping the essential. From discoveries sometimes follow great upheavals, and from the urge for a great transformation some-times follow new discoveries – both stimulate each other, creating a rhythm between the two poles.

In a trine, two closely related qualities form a friendship and support each other at all times: ideas are always fundamental and transform everything that has gone before; the fundamental expresses itself spontaneously and intense – the sudden is the essence of life.

In a sextile, two planets in zodiacal signs with different but similar qualities occa-sionally support each other: intuition has the possibility to grasp the essential, and the essence of all things has the possibility to (partially) show itself in spontaneous inspirations.

In a square one always checks anew in every situation which of the two qualities one wants to use – and the other quality stays completely out of it: spontaneity or essence, leap or transformation, inventor or magician.

In a quincunx, spontaneity and basic convictions always re-establish the order and the tension. This means that with every new invention and every new idea you have to see how it can be integrated into the whole, so that it serves the realization of the essential.

In a semi-sextile, either intuition or basic beliefs urge further development toward the other quality. Thus either the desire for something new gives way to the need for connection to the "root of life" (Uranus => Pluto) or one loses interest in the essential and prefers to simply experience something new (Pluto => Uranus).

IX 3. i) Neptune

Neptune – Pluto

In a conjunction one experiences no difference between boundary dissolution and the essential, since boundary dissolution is the essential. How else should art be able to attain depth, the human community be able to live in peace, God be able to be grasped as Creator, ecology be able to function?

In an opposition, one alternates rhythmically back and forth between fantasy and the existential, between symbiosis and grasping the essence. The contemplation of the essence leads to the fact that after a while one feels into the whole, which has emerged from the essence. Likewise, when one senses into the whole, after a while one begins to search for the common root of all the parts of the whole. Thus a rhythm arises between the essence and the whole that has emerged from that essence.

In a trine, two closely related qualities enter into a friendship and support each other at all times: sensing into the world makes it possible to grasp its roots and the seed from which they sprang. Community, mysticism, art, ecology and any form of boundary dissolution become the basic ingredients of life.

In a sextile, two planets in zodiacal signs with different but similar qualities occasionally support each other: the dissolution of boundaries can lead to the possibility of letting the essential become visible, and the essential can show itself in hunches.

With a square one always checks anew in every situation which of the two qualities one wants to use – and the other quality stays completely out of it: mysticism or magic, intuition or metamorphosis, leaping further development or new creation.

In a quincunx, boundary dissolution and essentials always re-establish order and tension. This leads to the question, where and when one can give oneself to the "floating in the big whole", and when one must concentrate on the essentials.

In a semi-sextile either the border resolution or the basic convictions push for a further development to the respective other quality. Thus either the desire for expansion gives way to the urge to live out of the essential (Neptune => Pluto) or the urge to live intensely fades and one simply wants to enjoy being one with everything (Pluto => Neptune).

IX Exercises

Astrology, like any other field of knowledge, becomes clearer and deeper and easier to apply by using it a lot.

1. Horoscopes

The most important way is simply to calculate and interpret many horoscopes.

There are many collections of horoscopes of well-known personalities on the Internet, which you can look at and compare – preferably the horoscopes of people about whom you already know something, such as politicians, sportsmen, actors, musicians, etc.

2. Types

You can also take a look at a book such as the seven "Harry Potter" volumes and see if you can identify what planetary or zodiac character certain characters have. You may also compare these characters with the horoskop of the quthor of that book.

A slightly different approach is to examine certain positions, for which soccer is particularly well suited. To begin with, this is very simple: find the birth dates of two dozen or more goalkeepers on the Internet and see if certain zodiac signs cluster among the goalkeepers. You can then do the same with the defenders, midfielders, forwards, liberos, and the like. This helps both to understand the positions in question and to understand the zodiac signs better.

3. Sun sign and ascendant

It is very helpful to look at the combinations of sun signs ("I am Virgo.") and ascendant. Again, one can take the help of the horoscopes of famous personalities available on the Internet. The sun sign and the ascendant are the two most influential elements in the horoscope, so a good understanding of these two elements is extremely beneficial.

The ascendant is the building material, so to speak, and the sun sign is the architect – the Ascendant is the style and the sun sign is the composer.

For example, Freud, being a Taurus, is interested in pleasure, and because of his Scorpio Ascendant, he explores the motivations of desire.

Karl Marx is also a Taurus and is therefore interested in possessions. However, because he has an Aquarius ascendant, he writes a theory of possession: "Capital."

Alfred Adler, a student of Freud, has a Scorpio ascendant, like his teacher, and therefore also has the same view on life: it's all about competition, envy, lack, struggle, and the like. However, being a Leo, he is not interested in the enjoyment of possessions like Freud the Taurus, but in self-expression, self-esteem, which is why he looks at the development and broadening of individuality – especially in sibling competition.

Another Freund disciple, C.G. Jung, like Alfred Adler, was a Leo. However, having an Aquarian ascendant like Karl Marx, he is not interested in competition for recognition like Alfred Adler, but instead outlines a theory of individuality in his writings.

Another worthwhile approach is to compare the (optical) appearance of people with the same zodiac sign (sun sign) or with the same ascendant, and preferably also of people with the same sun sign and ascendant combination (see my book "Photo-Astrologie").

4. Daily planetary position

There are websites available on the Internet that show the current planetary position. If you look at this planetary position every day and compare it with the events of that day, you will get a feeling for which constellations have which meaning.

5. Transits

A transit is a planet up in the sky, which is located where you have a planet in your horoscope. For example, if the current position of the Sun is 7° Pisces and you have Mercury at 7° Pisces in your chart, this transit makes your thinking (Mercury) more conscious and egocentric (Sun). So the planet in the horoscope gets a "coating" by the current planet at the same place in the zodiac up in the sky.

6. The personal astrological year calendar

Since the Sun is in the same place in the zodiac on the same day every year, a simple annual calendar can be created for each person, which shows what qualities the days in the year have. This individual, but lifelong constant yearly prediction is of course only related to the sun and does not take into account the other nine planets – so it is incomplete, but still useful.

This calendar has already been described in chapter "IV 2.".

7. Dream journeys

Finally, one can make dream journeys to the planets, the signs of the zodiac, the houses and the aspects. This method has the advantage that it is not based on understanding (Mercury), but on experiencing (Moon) and can therefore be a helpful second pillar in learning astrology.

X Further Considerations

This book only wants to give a first overview – that's why it is called "Astrology for Beginners". If you want to go further into one of these topics, you may find information about it in the following books:

Thomas Ring: "Astrologische Menschenkunde": an extensive and detailed presentation of all elements of horoscope astrology

Harry Eilenstein: "Astrologie": an introduction to astrology, aspect structure, combination of sun position and ascendant, differentiated presentation of the signs of the zodiac, worldview considerations, etc.

Harry Eilenstein: "Die Aspekte": an exact description of the aspects and their relations to each other

Harry Eilenstein: "Horoscop und Seele": a description of the relationship between soul and horoscope, from which it follows that the horoscope is the expression of the will of the soul, which in turn enables a different approach to one's own horoscope.

Harry Eilenstein: "Photo-Astrologie": 12 photos of men and 12 photos of women for each of the 144 sun-sign/ascendant combinations as well as for each planet in the 1st house

Harry Eilenstein: "Reinkarnation": an investigation whether reincarnation can be proved and what can be said about it and what results from it for astrology

Harry Eilenstein: "The Synthesis of Physics and Magic": among other things a description, in which form the zodiac and the astrological aspects are found in modern physics – among other things as Heisenberg's spin chain ("superstring") and as special angle relations in mechanics and electromagnetism

Altogether the astrological literature is almost multitudinous …

English Books by Harry Eilenstein

- Living Magic (261 p.)
- The Synthesis of Physics and Magic (192 p.)
- Telepathy for Beginners (60 p.)
- Telepathy for Advanced Learners (52 p.)
- Telekinesis for Beginners (56 p.)
- Life Force for Beginners (76 p.)
- Astral Projection for Beginners (60 p.)
- Meditation for Beginners (60 p.)
- Prophecy for Beginners (60 p.)
- Ritual Magic for Beginners (64 p.)
- Magic Chant for Beginners (108 p.)
- Invocations for Beginners (52 p.)
- Evocations for Beginners (62 p.)
- Auto-Movement for Beginners (60 p.)
- Elves for Beginners (56 p.)
- Hypnosis for Beginners (56 p.)
- Love Magic for Beginners (52 p.)
- Money Magic for Beginners (60 p.)
- Magic Objects for Beginners (64 p.)

- Shamanism for Beginners (52 p.)
- Self Knowledge for Beginners (60 p.)
- Astrology for Beginners (112 p.)
- Number Symbolism for Beginners (64 p.)
- Mandalas for Beginners (76 p.)
- Crop Circles for Beginners (344 p.)
- Feng Shui for Beginners (96 p.)

These books will be puplished soon:

- Kundalini for Beginners
- Chakra-Magic for Beginners
- Magic Research for Beginners
- Symbolism of Numbers for Beginners
- Language of the Moon – for Beginners
- Da'ath-Magic for Beginners
- Magic for Beginners – Anthology I
- Magic for Beginners – Anthology II
- Magic for Beginners – Anthology III
- Magic for Beginners – Anthology IV

Bücher von Harry Eilenstein

Religion allgemein
- Die sieben Schritte des Lebens (428 S.)
- Muttergöttin und Schamanen (168 S.)
- Göbekli Tepe (472 S.)
- Die Göttin von Göbekli Tepe (144 S.)
- Totempfähle (440 S.)
- Christus (60 S.)
- Dakini (80 S.)
- Vajra (76 S.)

Ägypten
- Hathor und Re 1: Götter und Mythen im Alten Ägypten (432 S.)
- Hathor und Re 2: Die altägyptische Religion – Ursprünge, Kult und Magie (396 S.)
- Isis (508 S.)

Indogermanen
- Die Entwicklung der indogermanischen Religionen (700 S.)
- Wurzeln und Zweige der indogermanischen Religion (224 S.)

Germanen
- Die Götter der Germanen (87 Bände – siehe nächste Seite)
- Odin (300 S.)

Kelten
- Cernunnos (690 S.)
- Taliesin (228 S.)
- Der Kessel von Gundestrup (220 S.)
- Der Chiemsee-Kessel (76)

Psychologie
- Über die Freude (100 S.)
- Das Geheimnis des inneren Friedens (252 S.)
- Das Beziehungsmandala (52 S.)
- Gefühle und ihre Verwandlungen (404 S.)
- einsgerichtet (140 S.)
- Liebe und Eigenständigkeit (216 S.)
- Von innerer Fülle zu äußerem Gedeihen (52 S.)

Heilung
- Die Symbolik der Krankheiten (76 S.)

Kunst
- Herz des Tanzes – Tanz des Herzens (160 S.)

Drama
- König Athelstan (104 S.)

Bücher von Harry Eilenstein

„Magie für Anfänger"

- Telepathie für Anfänger (60 S.)
- Telepathie für Fortgeschrittene (52 S.)
- Telekinese für Anfänger (52 S.)
- Lebenskraft für Anfänger (60 S.)
- Meditation für Anfänger (56 S.)
- Kundalini für Anfänger (100 S.)
- Hypnose für Anfänger (56 S.)
- Auto-Movement für Anfänger (56 S.)
- Chakra-Magie für Anfänger (148 S.)
- Astralreisen für Anfänger (56 S.)
- Astrologie für Anfänger (120 S.)
- Ritual-Magie für Anfänger (56 S.)
- Mandalas für Anfänger (68 S.)
- Geldzauber für Anfänger (56 S.)
- Liebeszauber für Anfänger (52 S.)
- Invokationen für Anfänger (52 S.)
- Evokationen für Anfänger (60 S.)
- Elfen für Anfänger (56 S.)
- Magie-Forschung für Anfänger (140 S.)
- Selbsterkenntnis für Anfänger (52 S.)
- Zahlensymbolik für Anfänger (60 S.)
- Die Sprache des Mondes – für Anfänger (116 S.)
- Zaubergesänge für Anfänger (100 S.)
- Zukunftschau für Anfänger (60 S.)
- Schamanismus für Anfänger (52 S.)
- Magische Gegenstände für Anfänger (68 S.)
- Da'ath-Magie für Anfänger (64 S.)
- Kornkreise für Anfänger (348 S.)
- Feng Shui für Anfänger (96 S.)
- Magie für Anfänger – Sammelband I (696 S.)
- Magie für Anfänger – Sammelband II (664 S.)
- Magie für Anfänger – Sammelband III (580 S.)

„Traumreisen"

- Traumreisen zu Heilpflanzen (700 S.)

Magie

- Handbuch für Zauberlehrlinge (408 S.)
- Tarot (104 S.)
- Physik und Magie (184 S.)
- Die Synthese von Physik und Magie (200S.)
- Die Magie-Formel (156 S.)
- Krafttiere – Tiergöttinnen – Tiertänze (112 S.)
- Schwitzhütten (524 S.)
- Mythen und Magie der Harfe (116 S.)
- Magie heute – Berichte aus der Praxis (288 S.)

Meditation

- Der Lebenskraftkörper (230 S.)
- Die Chakren (100 S.)
- Das Chakren-System mit den Nebenchakren (296 S.)
- Organe und Chakren (64 S.)
- Die platonischen Körper in den Chakren (156 S.)
- Meditation (140 S.)
- Drachenfeuer (124 S.)
- Kundalini I (676 S.)
- Reinkarnation (156 S.)
- einsgerichtet (140 S.)

Astrologie

- Astrologie (496 S.)
- Photo-Astrologie (428 S.)
- Die astrologischen Aspekte (88 S.)
- Horoskop und Seele (120 S.)

Kabbala

- Kursus der praktischen Kabbala (150 S.)
- Eltern der Erde (450 S.)
- Blüten des Lebensbaumes:
    - Die Struktur des kabbalistischen Lebensbaumes (370 S.)
    - Der kabbalistische Lebensbaum als Forschungshilfsmittel (580 S.)
    - Der kabbalistische Lebensbaum als spirituelle Landkarte (520 S.)

Die Themen der 87 Bände der Reihe „Die Götter der Germanen"